THE TEN MANAGEMENT PEPs

Plain English Principles for Being a Great People Manager

NIGEL JEREMY

Bloomington, IN

Milton Keynes, UK

AuthorHouse™
1663 Liberty Drive, Suite 200
Bloomington, IN 47403
www.authorhouse.com
Phone: 1-800-839-8640

AuthorHouse™ UK Ltd.
500 Avebury Boulevard
Central Milton Keynes, MK9 2BE
www.authorhouse.co.uk
Phone: 08001974150

First published by AuthorHouse 9/25/2006

ISBN: 1-4259-5321-2 (sc)

Printed in the United States of America
Bloomington, Indiana

This book is printed on acid-free paper.

To my mother, Marion, for her strength,
generosity, love and laughter;

and to my daughters Emma and Hannah
for the joy, the fun and the dance

- Nigel Jeremy

ACKNOWLEDGEMENTS

A number of special people have made contributions to the publication of this work. I am delighted to acknowledge their support in print.

Nicola, my wife, whose patience and constant support (...and coffee!) kept me sustained throughout the project.

Emma and Hannah, my daughters, who worked really hard to find and create suitable icons for each of the PEPs.

Thanks also to my friends and colleagues, Jonathan Crofts, David Scholey and Emma Jeffries who cheered me on and helped me out whenever times got tough.

Special thanks to my dear friend, Kay Collier, who acted as my literary advisor providing guidance, wise insight, direct feedback and unwavering support throughout.

CONTENTS

"Our deepest fear is not that we are inadequate, it's that we are powerful beyond measure..." (Marianne Williamson)

FOREWORD

Welcome to the world of Management "PEP"s, "Plain English Principles" to help you perform your critical management role.

Over the last twenty years, I have had the privilege of directly managing over 400 people across various industries and sectors, and the even greater honour of developing thousands of managers who want to become better at delivering the responsibilities and duties that come with the privilege of being a manager.

Over those two decades, just about every manager I've met has possessed drive and enthusiasm to be better at what they do. Interestingly, what being a better manager means to them often varies remarkably. But, whilst there are clear variations, there are also some very common themes which keep recurring.

The recurrence of these themes over thousands of conversations and indeed, over thousands of days gave rise to the simple, yet marvellously effective discoveries that this book will seek to articulate.

Specifically, my analysis of these experiences uncovered a set of core principles of management activity which, if applied consistently, will deliver successful managerial performance whether you're a first time supervisor or a CEO.

So if managers already possess drive and enthusiasm to be better, why do so many mess it up????????

There are many reasons for this but a recurring theme is that training and development plays a critical role here. Unfortunately, too often, managers find they have "more important things to do" or are not supported by their own managers to develop.

And even when support is available, those in the learning field (myself included) can have a tendency to overcomplicate issues with clever, innovative and insightful theory which managers see as complex, unworkable and unrealistic.

Clear and Present Danger

I'm sure you can imagine that, as a career learning professional, I've seen, read, experienced, and used a huge range of management and leadership theory over the years. Most of it has been interesting, much of it inspiring and there have even been a few things which I think were close to genius. I am a fan of theory, I like models, I like being able to explain why actions create reactions, why decisions create consequences, why our genetics and environment create behaviour patterns.

Despite my love of theory, I've become increasingly aware that there are some simple principles which, when done well, create highly satisfied, efficient, motivated individuals and teams which usually go on to deliver great results.

Equally, I've observed managers and teams where these principles were absent and, unsurprisingly, this has nearly always been coupled with demotivated individuals, dissatisfaction and poor team performance.

Management is no different to many things in life - get the basics right and success, if not inevitable, becomes so much easier to attain.

In my view, despite the best intentions, there is a clear and present danger emanating from HR departments worldwide to overcomplicate and hence confuse managers about the "right behaviour, right personality, right decision etc " often resulting in managers getting to a stage where the privilege of people management appears to be a huge and scary journey into a world of complex psychology, planning and decision making.

You know....sometimes, learning professionals just need to accept that being right and thorough in terms of managerial psychology and theory doesn't necessarily mean that managers can translate this into sound actions and decisions.

"I CAN'T SEE THE WOOD FOR THE TREES"

So you'll probably have already guessed that this is not a book about discovering who you are, or developing your ability to adapt who you are, or about a journey of self discovery.

This is a book about exposing the secrets of being a really effective manager by showing you the key things you need to do consistently and continuously to be an effective boss....and, trust me, it will work whether you're a newly appointed supervisor or the CEO of a major corporation.

Isn't there more to being a leader than following the 10 Plain English Principles (PEPs)?

The answer to this is absolutely YES. As I've mentioned, there are some great theories and models on Leadership out there. The approaches are many and varied but if I was looking for a simple description (and I am), the theories are often focused broadly around the concept of leadership being "management" plus the act of inspiring people to act and develop around a strategic vision and cause.

But try this as some food for thought:-

- Rarely do I see disenchanted followers talk about the lack of strategic inspiration from their bosses. Individuals are more concerned with the real daily experiences they share with their boss. They complain about senior and junior managers not doing "the simple things" consistently.
- I put to you that around 80% of your success as a manager or leader will come from effective use of the 10 PEPs
- Even better news is that these things should only take about 20-30% of your time

What, Why and How?

In each chapter, I'll seek to illustrate the "what" and the "why"(i.e. what the principle is and why it's important.)

As far as the "how" goes, here's the 50:50 deal.....

I'll provide tips to help you more easily carry out each principle but the other half of the "how" will be unique to you. I want you to think about executing the PEPs in your own unique way. You are an individual and have the right to behave, manage and lead others as you see fit as long as it's lawful, ethical and respectful.

So carry out each PEP in your own style ......but DO carry it out!!!!!

One last thing...

You may, like me, occasionally see things in the PEP that you feel are obvious or simplistic. If this happens, I challenge you to stop reading and seriously ask yourself these two questions:-

1) ***OK it's simple but do I really do this with my people consistently?***
2) ***What would my people privately say about how well I do this?***

..and don't beat yourself up if you haven't been doing these things. The fact that you're reading this now shows you are one of those managers who cares enough to spend time improving their ability to serve the people who serve them.

"Be the manager you can be and deal with your deepest fear.."

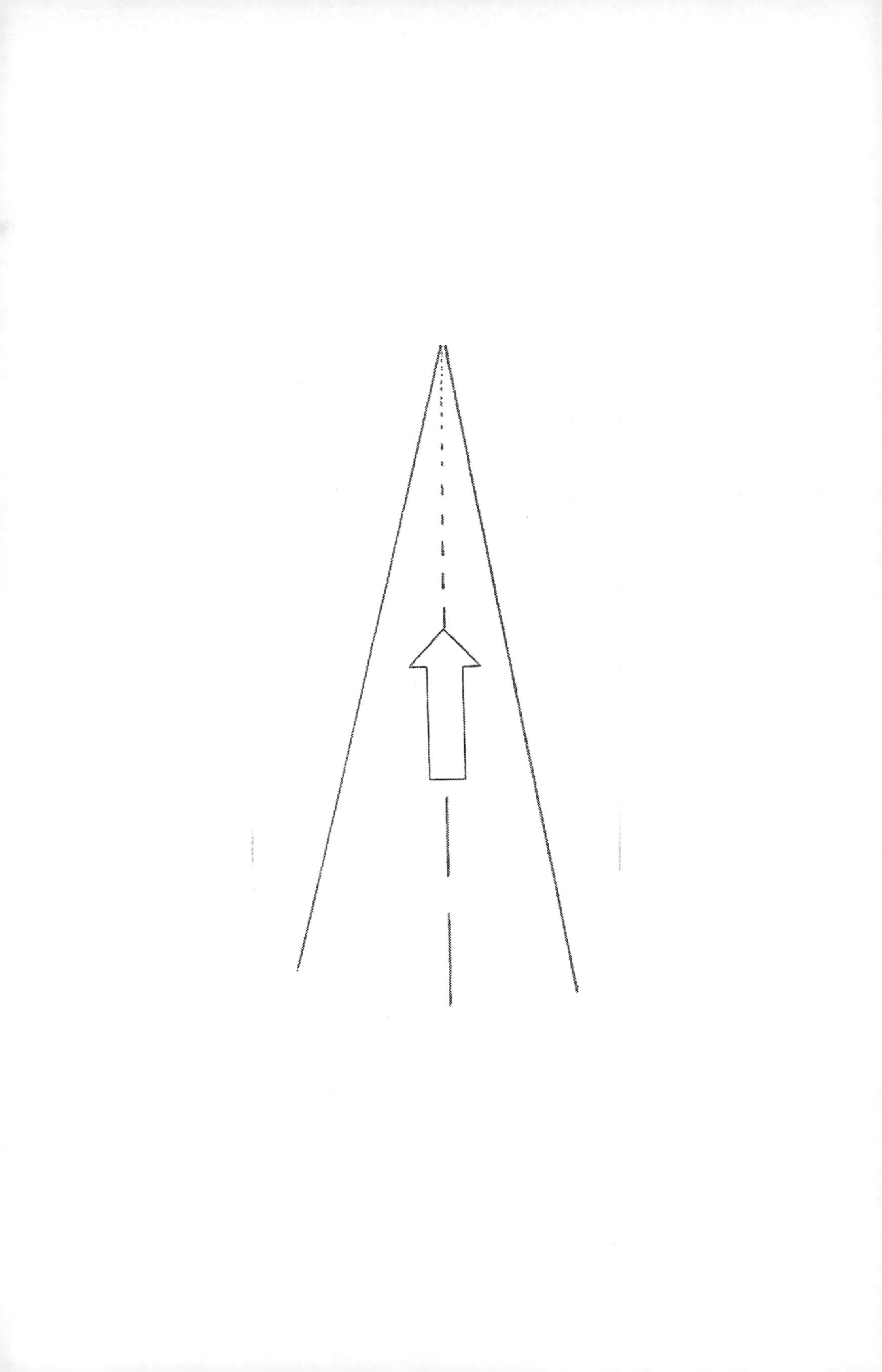

PEP 1

The Arrow Principle

SETTING CLEAR DIRECTION

Let's start with, what could appear to be, the blindingly obvious.

As a manager, it is your role to get the work of your area done through others – specifically, the people that report to you. So if you're managing a group of people, before any other big steps, you better be sure they are clear about what you expect of them.

Now, despite my best efforts, I've yet to find a genuine mind reader in business nor are crystal balls usually available in the stationery order. You can't expect people to somehow "know" what's expected unless you tell them. Equally, never expect people to perform if they don't know what you need them to do and the quality you need from them when they do it.

Most people are happy to be led. At the end of the day we all report to someone. Even the Chairman reports to the shareholders.

When being led, what people need, in business speak, is to be clear about their performance objectives* and understand how these broadly contribute to the overall success of the team or business.

Failure to set clear direction in this way can result in individuals becoming demotivated, creating their own agenda, poor individual and team output and a feeling of anarchy within the team. It can cause problems for customers and other teams who have to do business with you too.

But, by setting direction well, you take the first step to creating a team focused on performance by showing each of them clearly what you and they need to achieve to be successful.

*Objectives are also called targets, KPIs (key performance indicators), goals, and stretch goals in the mad language of business

"People, like nails, lose their effectiveness when they lose direction and begin to bend"
(Walter Savage Landor)

Ok – How Do I Know What Objectives To Use?

There are many options. You can get really grandiose and look at organisation mission, values and your department's business strategy and these will certainly help give you the context in which you operate.

But if you really want to cut to the chase, how about starting with **your** role description and the objectives **you've** been set by your boss.

If these aren't available (i.e. don't exist) then book a meeting with your boss to discuss and develop your objectives. Don't whinge if he or she hasn't had the foresight to do it already, draw a line in the sand and say to yourself, the good practice starts here and take control of the situation.

"Managers get the work done through others"
"What gets measured gets done"

Using your own role description and objectives provides you with the broad direction you need to set for your team members. Your task now is to translate your objectives into something meaningful for each of your team members. Break each objective down into more detail and be more specific about the action each individual needs to take.

A full set of objectives would usually cover each of the following areas

People objectives – how you expect each of your people to develop, to work as a team, to come prepared for 1-1s and how they manage others (if they are people managers too).

Customer Service objectives – what standards do they need to deliver

Compliance objectives– key operational processes, rules they have to follow

End results – what are the final results you expect from their activity

How Do I Set An Objective?

There are various models out in the market giving you a structure for writing objectives. Most are thorough and grounded in good science but managers often complain that it takes forever to develop objectives in these ways.

The three key things about creating a workable and useful objective

1. Ensure the objective is described in a way that can be broadly understood by the individual
2. Show how and when you will measure success – this is the critical element as it will clarify to the individual what you need from them.
3. Involve the individual in creating the objective, it helps get *buy-in*

When writing your objectives, I recommend you connect points 1 and 2 together with the words "evidenced by"

e.g. – Deliver a high level of customer service **evidenced by** achieving 70% or over on your personal rating from monthly mystery shopper results.

"Show me the measure, I'll show you the objective"

The objective is clear and succinct. Mystery shopper standards can be provided separately and don't need to be recorded on the objectives document. Remember, the key thing is that the individual is clear on what's required – you don't need "War and Peace" on a document to create the clarity.

Caramel Objectives

***"the Lords Prayer has 56 words;
the Ten Commandments has 297;
the American Declaration of Independence has 300;
but a European directive on the import of caramel and caramel products requires 26,911 words.
The moral is obvious."
(Sir Frank Hartley)***

How many objectives?

The rule of thumb here is to set enough objectives to cover the key areas of the role description and the 4 areas outlined earlier (people, customers, compliance, end results) but not so many that the individual gets lost in a sea of targets not knowing where to focus.

Given the above I tend to recommend a range with a minimum of 8 objectives and maximum of 16 objectives. Your call.

Record Keeping

Keep a record of the objectives on file and ensure your team member gets a copy. The list of objectives needs to be a true living document. This is critical as it's essential to the delivery of PEPs 2, 3, 5 and 7. The list of objectives is the first page in your "performance file" for each individual.

Changing objectives

Times change and the business moves on. You'll often find yourself needing to update objectives with your people. Never be frightened to change, delete or add objectives – just be sure to discuss what you want to change with the individual and then record what you've done on their performance file.

Of course, keeping an up to date record of objectives for each individual is obvious isn't it??

I wonder how many managers do it and then leave it in the file, gathering dust to the next annual performance review??

What do <u>you</u> think?

Top Tips – The Arrow Principle

- People are not mind readers – tell them what you expect
- Involve your people in setting their objectives
- Set direction through objectives
- Use your role description and objectives as a starting point and translate
- Spread objectives across the areas of people, customer service, compliance and end results
- Don't "caramelise" your objectives
- The measure specifies the objective – use "evidenced by"
- Start a performance file by keeping a record of the objectives you've agreed. Keep it live

"Objectives are not fate, they are direction. They are not commands, they are commitments"
(Peter Drucker)

So I guess that's all there is to it. You can now go back to your desk having set the direction for your team members. All they have to do now is do what you've agreed and they'll bring the results in.

Just let them know where you'll be if they have any questions and success is inevitable - **right?**

WRONG!!!

PEP 1 is just the beginning. Once your people know what you want, you then need to find a way to make them believe you really mean it when you say these objectives are important.

They need to feel you are with them on the journey rather than presiding over your empire

They need to be helped, cajoled, thanked for good work and "guided" when they go off track.

And you need to do these things in a way that allows you to be true to yourself as well as giving you enough time to continue to enjoy life.

This is where the other PEPs come in...

PEP 2

The Daily Principle

JUST IN TIME FEEDBACK

Everyone has an invisible sign hanging around their neck saying "make me feel important" - always remember that when working with people (anon)

This principle is about the things you should do with your people every single day of the week.

Whilst PEP 1 (The Arrow Principle), enables your people to be clear about what you expect of them, the Daily Principle works to re-enforce the importance of these objectives being met and acts as a motivator to the individuals to achieve them.

So what are the things you should make a point of discussing with your people every day.........

Praising and Challenging
Praising good performance and behaviour and reprimanding the bad.

Sharing and Guiding
Exchanging information and answering questions

Bonding and Laughing
Showing you care and having some fun

Let's break these down a little further.....

Praising and Challenging

You might sometimes hear this called "in the moment" feedback. "In the moment" means real time, as it happens (or very quickly after it happens).

It needs to be done as often as situations arise. On some days this could be 2 or 3 times, on others none at all. Let circumstances dictate when you do this rather than looking to do it x times per day or week.

What is it?

Praising – if you see someone doing something really well, tell them, thank them, congratulate them.

Challenging – conversely, if you see someone doing something badly, tell them and help them see another way.

9 basic rules for praising and challenging

1. Do it privately (especially challenging).
2. Praise/challenge the result or the behaviour never the individual.
3. Be reasonably specific about what you saw or heard.
4. Talk about how it made you feel (proud, delighted, happy, disappointed, angry, frustrated).
5. Don't make up excuses to praise or challenge – be genuine.
6. Don't make a drama out of it – say what you have to say and move on.

7. When challenging, work with the individual to help them avoid the situation in future.

8. Be yourself, use your own style. Forcing a behaviour will tend to make you feel and look awkward.

9. Make a note in the "performance file" if you feel appropriate.

SHARING AND GUIDING

You will frequently get information that you need to share quickly with your people. Mostly, this will be about specific tasks they need to perform but, occasionally, you may also just want to share some stuff about a bigger issue or a bit of interesting news.

Equally, your team members may need and want to share information with you like updating you on progress or asking you questions.

So don't always wait for a 1-1 or team meeting, get out with your people, have a chat with them and interact **throughout** the day.

BONDING AND LAUGHING

Look, we spend more of our waking hours in work than with our families.

So, as the boss, try as far as you can to help make work an enjoyable experience for both yourself and your people.

Having a chat with them about what they did at the weekend, a hobby or a shared interest, a joke or a funny story shows that you care and value them as people and not just a work resource.

There will be times to be serious but, trust me, people work for people and they like their bosses to be human. As long as you don't overplay this element, it's an amazingly disarming and motivational thing to do.

Everyone has an invisible sign hanging around their neck saying "make me feel important" - always remember that when working with people

So the bottom line is… get out amongst your people daily, being seen to care about how work is progressing and how they are getting on with life generally.

It's also about being fair and balanced between recognising good performance and being seen to deal with bad performance. This reminds your people that the direction you've set remains important to you.

Being You

To some of you, The Daily Principle may seem right up your street. You know, those of you that think you've got the "gift of the gab", can already see yourselves getting around your people, ducking and diving, being really dynamic, entertaining them with bit of banter ……

To others, it may appear quite scary because what I've described above isn't your natural style. You prefer to be less open or gregarious.

As human beings, we all fall into the trap of sometimes stereotyping behaviour and making assumptions that certain behaviours go hand in hand with certain activities. Sometimes this is true, but most of the time it isn't.

"There's more than one way to skin a cat"

The Daily Principle can be accomplished equally as effectively…

..whether you're quiet, reserved, shy and softly spoken

OR

..whether you're gregarious, loud, socially outgoing and openly confident.

Do it your way.

Hmmmm…..Still need convincing?

Let me briefly illustrate by way of some example dialogue using different styles in a praising situation.

Be Big, Be Bold, He Who Dares Wins

"Hey Jack, just saw your last report. Looks fantastic! I loved the bit where you showed those extra savings. Brilliant! Wonderfully impressive. (arm around or pat on the shoulder). Good job!"

Walk Softly and Carry a Big Stick

"Hi Jack, I've just read you're last report. I think this is a really strong piece of work. I was really impressed by the savings you showed at the same time as increasing the quality of production. Thanks Jack, (strong eye contact and smile) I just wanted you to know how pleased I was with your work on this."

And for you, the style could be somewhere between the two. You also have the choice whether to do this verbally or in writing; in public or in private.

Locard's Principle

This is the law of forensic science which simply states

"Every contact leaves a trace"

I'm sure that you can see how this principle may be directly applied to your management style. Every interaction you have with your people will leave a trace, an impression and cause a reaction

In your interactions you need to be mindful of the "trace" that you want to leave behind with your people. Above all, the important thing is to do what comes naturally in terms of who you are and be consistent in your behaviour.

Being Consistent

People quickly catch onto the personality of their boss and particularly like thinking they can, at least partly, predict how you might react to most work situations.

When your behaviour is fairly consistent, it helps your people translate what you're saying about something, how important it is and how passionate you are about it.

Your consistency provides them with a "boss normal" benchmark which they can then adapt to and appreciate over time. Also, when you deviate from "normal", they quickly notice. If used with care this can be a very powerful management aid for you.

Don't Be a Flipper

People hate working for "flippers" - Those managers who regularly "flip" their behaviour for no apparent reason.

People who work for a flipper can quickly become de-motivated and stressed as they can't predict how their boss will react in a given situation. Most of the time this is accompanied by whisperings like *"the boss is having one of his/her off days again, keep your head down"*. And the team start keeping out of their manager's way.

The boss will also start losing credibility as "flipping" usually appears very irrational to onlookers and will be stereotyped as emotional or moody or just plain "barking-mad" by their team and peers alike.

Kind of hard to keep the respect of your team if you behave like this don't you think?

Trying out new approaches

The whole purpose of learning is to be able to see, do, or consider something in a different way. We have to learn in order to develop ourselves as people.

Like I said, being yourself and being consistent in your behaviour is key to executing the Daily Principle well but…….

….at the same time, don't be frightened about trying something a bit different to what you've done before. Sometimes, you don't know you can really do something until you try it.

Your checks on this are:

- If you think you can do it and you want to try it, then **try it.**
- If you're unsure whether you can do it but still want to try it, then **try it** (with someone you know and trust well).
- Don't leap from one behaviour to the extreme opposite – **take small steps.**
- If you're uncomfortable about it – **don't do it** .

"Whether you think you can or whether you think you can't, you're right!" (Henry Ford)

The third point on small steps is really important. Nothing will lose you credibility with your people faster than having an overnight *"personality transplant"*.

I've seen managers with quieter and more reserved personalities turning up for work after being away on a course trying to be "the life and soul of the party". Pretending to be something their not and looking very foolish and creepy when putting an arm awkwardly around someone's shoulder and looking manically enthusiastic.

I've also seen loud and gregarious managers returning from courses trying to be "serious and sincere" but coming across as way too intense or completely patronising, condescending and shallow.

So, by all means, try new approaches when you want to but always take small steps and avoid trying anything that makes you feel awkward.

BEING AUTHENTIC

"You are an individual and have the right to behave, manage and lead others as you see fit as long as it's lawful, ethical and respectful"

To lead your people consistently and effectively, you need to be true to yourself whilst finding a way to create a connection or common ground with them.

So, people will tend to like you, respect you and think you sincere if you act and behave in a way consistent with your real personality.

When you couple this with making some adjustments allowing for the personality of the person or people you are interacting with, then you are on the road to demonstrating great leadership qualities

This balance of being many things to many people whilst staying true to yourself is often called **being authentic.**

"Be yourself – who is better qualified?"
(Frank J Giblin II)

"To be yourself in a world that is constantly trying to make you something else is the greatest accomplishment"
(Ralph Waldo Emerson)

Top Tips for the Daily Principle

- ❑ Make time to do this every day
- ❑ Make your people feel important
- ❑ Show the direction you've set remains important to you
- ❑ Interact with each of your people at least once every day
- ❑ Use all key types of interaction:
    - Praise and Challenge them
    - Share with them and Guide them
    - Bond and Laugh with them
- ❑ Try new approaches but take small steps
- ❑ Don't be a flipper
- ❑ Every contact leaves a trace – chose what trace you want to leave
- ❑ Be yourself. Be consistent. Be Authentic

"Do it your own way but do do it !!"

SUCCESS
CITY
75 miles

PEP 3

The Milestone Principle

MONTHLY 1-1S

So you've set direction and are now talking to your teams members every day about progress and the other things we covered in PEP 2.

The Milestone Principle is about the simple process of booking and CARRYING OUT regular 1:1 meetings with each of your direct reports through the year.

The 1:1 has two broad purposes:

Directional purpose – it's a FORMAL opportunity for you to jointly review the individual's performance, work progress, future plans and development needs

Emotional purpose – it's a PRIVATE opportunity for you to get to know and understand each other better. It provides a routine setting where you can be "intimate" and more honest and open with each other than you can usually be in the open workplace.

Most people understand the directional bit, it's the stuff that management is expected to cover right?

The emotional bit is always worthy of a bit more explanation.

When it comes to motivating your people (which we'll cover in PEP 4), understanding your people, their dreams, fears, likes, dislikes, life situation etc. is important. It's important because knowledge of an individual allows you to say or do things in a way which will get the best out of them.

So the emotional part of the 1-1 is a critical element and you should use this scarce time together to create a positive and healthy working relationship. Honesty, integrity, laughter, care, sensitivity, straight talking, listening, being interested are the watchwords of behaviour here.

The 1-1s are a key structural pillar in creating a highly performing team as they provide a formal routine for managers to talk to each team member about:

- their performance to date
- future performance requirements
- issues affecting the individual
- support needed by the individual to deliver their goals.

Milestone?

I'm often asked how often should 1-1s be done. As a rule of thumb, I've always found a **monthly** frequency highly effective. I've seen managers do this every 2 months and it's clearly not enough to have discussions like this once every 9/10 weeks, you simply lose touch with what's going on.

Equally, I've seen managers have weekly or fortnightly 1-1s and the converse is true. There's too little to talk about, it wastes time and can start to make the 1-1 a bit of a joke for all involved. The only time I'd recommend weekly or fortnightly 1-1s is for an intense working period like a major project launch or an underperformance issue but this frequency should be used only for special short term situations.

Quite simply, through having a regular, MONTHLY 1-1, you are inviting your team to believe you care about them and the progress they are making towards the direction you've set. A monthly frequency gives you enough of a gap between meetings for there to be enough "meat" in your discussion and each 1-1 acts as a true "Milestone" in the performance year. Monthly also gives you enough of a "breathing space" between discussing the more personal issues impacting the individual.

How Long Should A 1-1 Last?

The churlish answer is "as long as it needs to".

But you've got a business to run and a diary to manage right, so let's get real.

One hour is usually enough to cover everything if you're meeting monthly. You will need to flex time between the 4 areas as needed by you or your team member and occasionally you might go slightly over time. If you do run over, you'll have to make the call to continue there and then or book an extra 15 minutes in later in the day or week. If this happens, make sure you get the extra time together, it's very important to them and could be very important to you.

How To Conduct A 1-1

Before we get into this, please follow this tip - **Take brief notes throughout the 1-1** - it will help you recall things as the hour progresses and provide you with a record of the 1-1 you can keep on the performance file for future reference.

OK, let's split the 1-1 down into its component parts and take each one in turn. As you read on, remember that we are looking for a blend of direction and emotion.

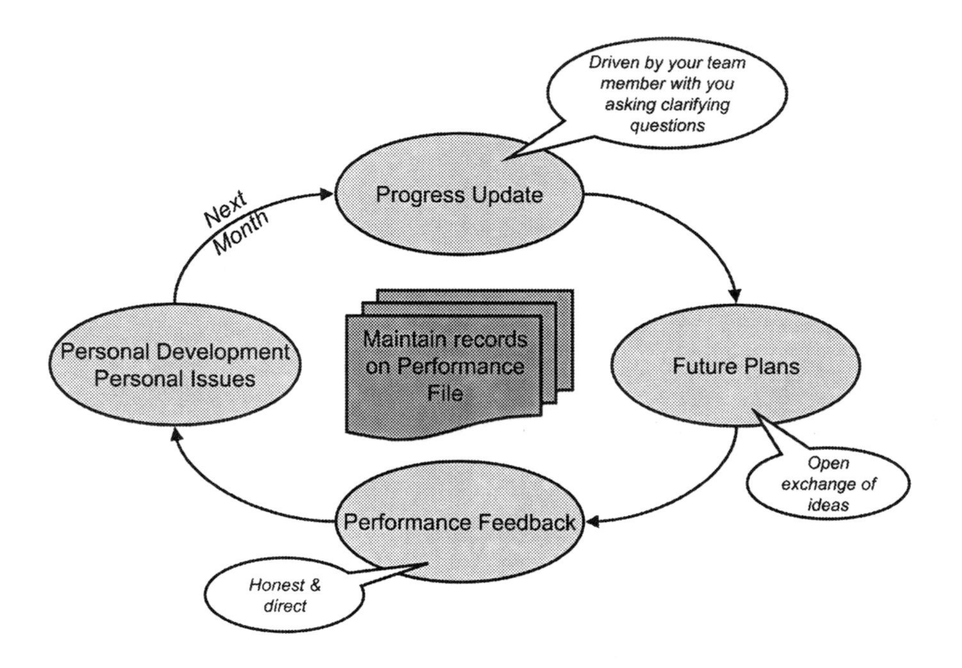

Part 1 - Progress Update

A really simple way is to ask your staff member to bring a copy of their performance objectives to every 1-1, together with a summary update that they can talk through with you.

This will provide a good structure for your discussion, act as a reminder to you both on the direction set and give you clues as to whether any new objectives should be set through the year.

That's all there is to this bit. Listen, ask questions to clarify and make notes!

Part 2 - Future plans

The progress update can give you clues and ideas for new activity during the 1-1 but you should also prepare in advance. You may have information on a new project that you haven't shared yet, or you may want to adjust an existing objective. Think about it before the 1-1 so that you don't miss the opportunity to discuss it.

Additionally, during the 1-1 you may well get into a discussion about your staff member's ideas for improving team performance and a new objective may emerge. It doesn't always have to be your idea so take the time to have a discussion when this occurs and agree the objective there and then if you think it's useful. (and recording it in the individual's performance file)

I guarantee it will make your staff member feel great as they'll rightly believe they've been really listened to and made a real contribution.

If you don't think the idea has merit, tell them why not and give them the opportunity to challenge you. It's your decision ultimately so what have you got to lose by allowing them to challenge you a little.

I often find a "let me think about it" response works well if I'm not sure so I can consider the idea for a bit longer before agreeing whether to support it or not. This way, if the news is good, the individual is happy, if the news is bad, then the individual at least knows you gave it some thought and you've been able to prepare the reasons behind your decision more carefully.

Part 3 - Performance Feedback

This can come out partially during the progress update bit but it's always useful to have a slightly more formal few minutes in the 1-1 where you can cover the positive and not so positive stuff. Your people like to know where they stand with you and how you think they are performing generally as well as specifically on certain activities.

It's critical you are honest and open in this section. Briefly review some of the "praising and challenging" situations that have occurred, give an indication of the extent of your satisfaction with their performance.

- If you are happy with their performance, then for goodness sake TELL THEM – it's so simple and people love to hear it (just don't get all mushy on them).
- If you have mild concerns, talk about them in a positive way with a view to finding a solution through discussion with your team member.
- If you have more serious concerns, then a different approach will be needed (refer to PEP 7 for this later).

Generally, the same broad principles apply here as we use for Praising and Challenging. (covered in the PEP 2 - Daily Principle)

Oh….. and don't forget to record a summary of the feedback you've given and place it in the performance file you started during PEP 1!

Part 4 - Personal issues and development

This is where you really move into the relationship side of the 1-1. Throughout the discussion, you may be receiving clues about where the individual needs help in improving their performance. This is the point where you bring these clues together and talk to the individual about ways you and others like the training department can help. The accent should be mainly on your support as the leader, coach and mentor for the individual.

The development you discuss doesn't just have to be due to the individual demonstrating performance gaps. It may be about developing something that's already good into a strength or helping the individual develop for future career moves.

This is also the time when you talk to the individual about "any other issues" they may want to discuss. Believe me, the responses can be hugely varied and sometimes surprising. It's important to cover this in your 1-1 as it completes the current picture of where the individual "is at" and helps you develop your relationship.

Here's a small list of things I've been on the receiving end of in 1-1s

Just wanted to remind you I'm on holiday for the next 2 weeks…
I'm having some trouble with the kids at the moment
I'm getting married
My father's really poorly
Fancy a beer on Friday
My wife's left me
I'm having a baby !!
I've got cancer
I want to apply for this job
I'm emigrating

There can be a huge spectrum and you should be prepared for the one's where you need to be more careful with your response. You'll often pick up some of the good and not so good personal stuff through the Daily Principle but you'd be surprised how often team members feel the need to tell their boss something before anyone else.... and wait for the 1-1 to do it!

Your people tell you these intimate things as they are connecting them to the work situation - and you're their leader in work. Your reaction needs to reflect what you're being told and then be followed with a discussion around how you can help from a work context (after the *I'm really sorry to hear that* or *That's fantastic news!* type of initial response).

Think about the situations I've mentioned - how would you **like** to have reacted if you had been there instead of me?

Just reflect on that for a moment before reading on...

Remember to be yourself – Stay lawful, ethical and respectful **by being prepared so you can react effectively.** This becomes more important with the sensitivity of the issue. By being you and also sharing something of yourself when you feel appropriate you create a strengthening bond essential for a great working relationship.

Continue to make brief notes in this bit of the 1-1 too, taking particular care with sensitive information.

"The emotional part of the 1-1 is a critical element and you should use this scarce time together to create a positive and healthy working relationship. Honesty, integrity, laughter, care, sensitivity, straight talking, listening, being interested are the watchwords of behaviour here."

Top Tips – The Milestone Principle

- Book one hour 1-1s with each of your team every month
- Make sure you carry out the 1-1s – never cancel at last minute
- Carry out the 1-1 in private as far as your work premises allow (an office or meeting room is ideal)
- Use it for directional and emotional (motivational) purposes
- Cover the 4 elements in each 1-1:
    - Progress update
    - Future Plans
    - Performance Feedback
    - Personal issues and development
- Record a summary of what was discussed and keep it in the individual's performance file
- If you run out of time, schedule extra time to complete the discussion and be sure to keep the appointment
- Be yourself
- Be prepared so you can react effectively

PEP 4

The Loving Principle

MOTIVATING YOUR PEOPLE

"In order to motivate your people effectively, you have to love them at least a little"

The Oxford English Dictionary defines motivation as

1) giving a person a reason or motive for doing something
2) making a person determined to achieve something

I prefer the following definition :-

Motivation is about getting people to willingly do, to the best of their ability, what needs to be done.

The Loving principle sets out how you go about keeping your people energised and positive and even excited about working towards the objectives you've agreed with them. That is – how you motivate your people to achieve the results you need from them.

Doesn't this all sound a bit familiar, haven't we already covered this?

Yes, we've covered **some** of the processes that help you with this in the earlier PEPs. Indeed, by the time you complete this book, you'll see that all the Principles make some contribution to the motivation of your people.

What's special about PEP4 is that it's the chapter where we'll explore, with a light touch, some of the psychology of motivation you need to be aware of as a manager. The chapter will also contain tips on how you can create a climate of motivation within your team using this new found awareness.

Ultimately, this knowledge will assist you in the task of motivation and help you put in context why some of the other PEPs work effectively in the overall running of your team.

Are you ready?

LIGHT TOUCH PSYCHOLOGY

There has been some truly excellent work done in the field of motivational psychology over the last century. Amongst my favourite exponents are Maslow, Herzberg, McGregor and Vroom.

The reason I like their work is a very practical one. Whilst their theories and concepts were rigorous, clever, complex and research based, they all possess the delightful property of being able to be "boiled down" into some simple key components that can be easily explained to managers and, most importantly, easily remembered and used by managers in daily interactions with their people.

The four key components that follow are my attempt at translating some of their work into simple tips that you can use every day.

KEY COMPONENTS

1) All people have a hierarchy of personal needs that they are motivated towards achieving[1]. The higher level needs only tend to become active as the lower level needs are satisfied. The personal needs, from highest to lowest are:

- Self Actualisation - Feeling of fulfilment. Need for personal development, challenge, creative expression.
- Esteem/Respect - Feeling others acknowledge the worth of what you do and who you are. Excelling in order to gain recognition and status.

---

[1] Maslow, A.H.(1943) A Theory of Human Motivation. Psychological Review, 50(4) 370-396

- Love/Belonging - Feeling accepted as part of a group, family, friends. The need for affection and friendship.
- Safety/Security - Hanging onto and protecting what you already have. Safety from emotional as well as physical injury.
- Physiological/Survival - Need for food, shelter, warmth, health.

So, individuals within a team can be at different levels of the hierarchy at different times. Through this simple truth, I've seen managers adjust their approach and hugely impact team motivation.

How?

If individuals in your team are motivated by different needs then you need to think about what **they** need before you open your mouth in an attempt to motivate them. This means you have to find out a bit more about your people - their life situation, pressures, dreams and aspirations.

The good news is that, if you're following the Daily and Milestone Principles, you already should be picking up this information anyway. Now you need to use it. Let's use a few very positive examples to illustrate:-

Safety/Physiological – (Needs job security, food, shelter, warmth)

"That's great Kay, you really are vital to this team, this business needs more people like you. Keep it up!!"

Love/Belonging – (Needs to feel liked by others and be part of a team)

"Great work Kay, can't believe you've managed to navigate through all the bureaucracy. You fit in so well with the others in the team and I keep getting feedback on what a good team player you are. I think you're able to get through all this stuff because of the great relationships you're clearly forming. Keep it up!!"

Esteem – (Needs to feel respected by others for the quality and quantity of their work)

"Great work Kay, awesome! You're setting the standard for others to follow. In fact, would you mind helping out Hannah and show her how you go about……, I know she'd really appreciate help from you"

2) The satisfaction of some needs doesn't actually motivate people. But, if these needs aren't satisfied, huge demotivation or dissatisfaction can result.

Herzberg calls these dissatisfiers, hygiene factors[2]. These things that must be present in order to get you to the starting line on motivating people.

Hygiene Factors

- Physical work environment – temperature, comfort, noise, safety etc
- Context in which work is done – policies, resources, time pressures, culture etc

[2] Herzberg, F. Mausner, B and Snyderman, BB (1959) – The Motivation to Work 2nd Edition

Herzberg also suggested there were other factors associated with feelings of satisfaction that did motivate. He called these satisfiers or motivators

Motivating Factors

- Interesting/Challenging work
- Responsibility
- Achievement
- Recognition
- Advancement

The learning I take here is that you must take care of these hygiene factors before anything else. This can be related to Maslow's theory because Herzberg essentially maintains that only higher level needs are motivators and that meeting lower level needs merely provides fulfilment of hygiene factors i.e. gets you to the starting line of motivating your people.

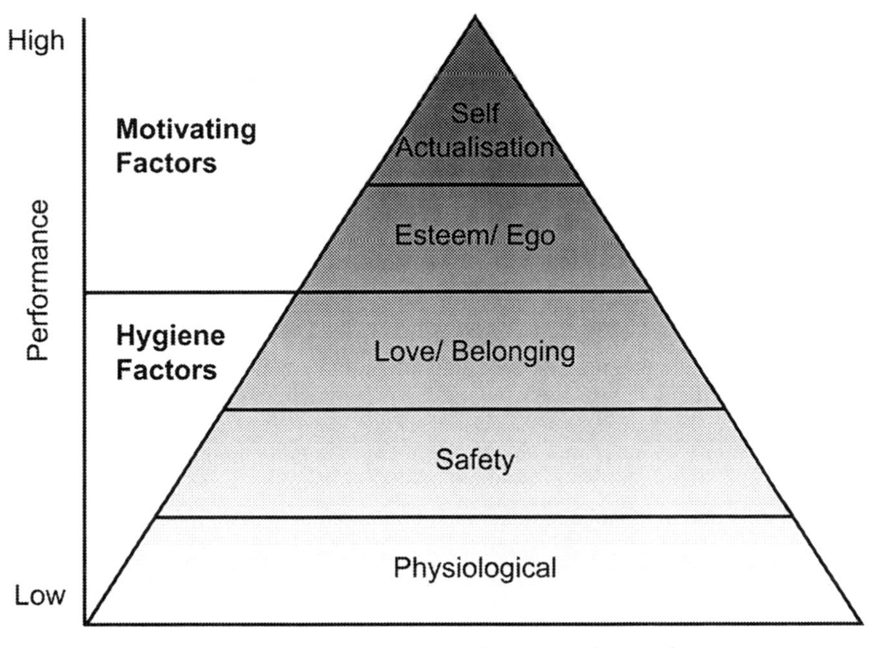

The link between Herzberg and Maslow

The "level" a person needs motivating at can vary over days, weeks and months. So, if you are used to working at the Esteem level in your discussions with an individual, your style will have less impact than usual if the toilets are broken or the person is worried about their workload or their bills or the office is way too hot or cold. Get these things sorted where they are within your control and adjust your motivational style down the hierarchy so you don't demotivate your people.

3) The intensity of a person's motivation to do what you need depends on their belief that they will get what they need if they do what you need.

Vroom[3] said that this intensity is affected by:

- Their desire for a certain outcome if they do it.
- The effort they think they have to put in to achieve it.
- Their belief that by doing it, the outcome they desire will be achieved.

For example:

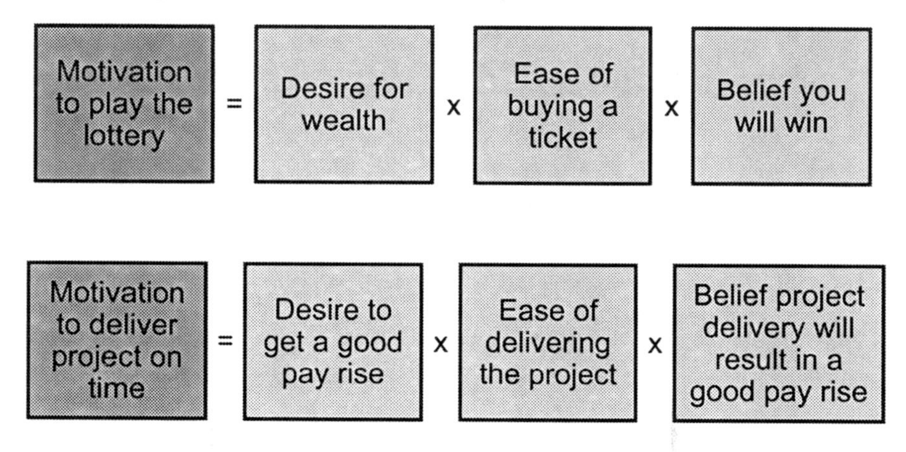

The point here is that you need to consider these three factors when considering your approach. If the desire or the belief is too low, or the effort is too great something needs to change.

This is totally situational so if you think there's a problem discuss it with the individual and see if a way can be found to put an extra ingredient in that will make the above equation workable for them and you.

---

[3] Victor Vroom, Work and Motivation (1964)

4) Managers can better motivate if they treat their people as responsible and valued employees[4]

Douglas McGregor formulated two theories of behaviour of individuals at work. Theory X suggests people inherently dislike working and prefer to be directed and controlled. Theory Y suggests people view work as being as natural as play and rest and will naturally exercise self control and accept responsibility.

The thing I find most interesting is that whichever of the above theories a manager most believes, this will lead them to behave in a way that creates the employee attitude linked to the particular theory.

In my view, this links to the age old story of the carrot and the stick approach to motivation and you'll notice that I've mainly focussed on a carrot style (Y) approach in this PEP. There's a very good reason for that.

People can be motivated by the stick (X). A "just do it" style, management through fear, rudeness, bullying, keeping people "on their toes" with aggressive questioning and unrealistic demands can all get the job done. However, this style is a bit like a firework. Lot's of noise and sparks, satisfying for a short time but then ......nothing but debris and a nasty smell of gunpowder.

"By the stick" is very short sighted, unethical and manifests itself as poor management and business practice. It results in medium and long term demotivation, is a major barrier to growing the potential of your people over time and can cause long term employee disengagement within the business. In short, a recipe for disaster.

"You do not lead by hitting people over the head – that's assault, not leadership" (Dwight D. Eisenhower)

[4] Douglas McGregor, The Human Side of Enterprise (1960)

The carrot, by contrast, is like a log fire. It can take a little time and patience to get going but once started, it can keep warm forever as long as it's regularly tendered.

The "carrot approach" is about nurturing, encouraging and empowering your people to be the best they can be. It takes time and patience but having motivated, capable, happy and talented people working in your team will deliver immense rewards for you, for them and for the business.

You might remember we talked about Praising and Challenging in the Daily Principle. Both these actions should usually be done in a "carrot style" even though challenging is essentially a reprimand.

So the bottom line on this is focus on the carrot style of motivation. Use the stick style only when you feel there is no other option. Never, ever let the stick become your normal style. It's bad for you, your people and your business.

So lets put this all together

The Four Components:

- All people have a hierarchy of personal needs that they are motivated towards achieving.
- Satisfying some needs only gets you to the starting line of motivating your people (Hygiene factors).
- The intensity of a person's motivation to do what you need depends on their belief that they will get what they need if they do what you need.
- Managers can better motivate if they treat their people as responsible and valued employees (use the carrot not the stick).

These four components are what make up the "light touch theory" I mentioned at the start of PEP4. The stuff I've covered here should be all the theory you really need to be a motivational manager, leave the rest to the psychologists and HR people!

Seriously though, this should cover you for most day to day issues. I'd recommend you read more about the work of my favourite exponents listed at the beginning of this PEP when you have more time after finishing this book. They published some really interesting stuff.

So what now?

You'll already have gathered that motivation is about how you do things not what you do. In the earlier PEPs, I've regularly covered the importance of "being yourself". Nothing changes here, except you now have some further information to help you when you are interacting with your people.

The most positive interactions take place when you communicate authentically AND take into account the person with whom you are communicating.

This needs merely a thought just before you speak with someone or even while you are speaking with someone.

The Thought

"Am I really motivating them here – what do they need from me?"

Just asking yourself this question will help you make the small adjustments in what you are saying. Believe me, it can be done in the moment, it just takes a bit of practice.

And, as ever, less is more. Take small steps rather than massive leaps to motivate your team members. Small steps keep the change sustainable and avoid generating the suspicion you've had a personality transplant.

Breaking a taboo

I want to cover something now that you might feel a little controversial. It's the issue of how close a leader should get to their people. I have met plenty of managers both successful and not who have said something like this….

"you know, being a manager can be a lonely place. You have to stay a little apart from the troops, familiarity breeds contempt and they always need to know who is the boss. There needs to be a demarcation and a line they can't cross so you can carry out your role as a manager effectively"

I could go on and on, but I'm sure you get the message. Here's my response....

"whilst the belief - ***it's better to stay apart*** *- is understandable, it's not essential. You have a choice in these things and every choice has consequences. Ask yourself if it's more about feeling secure in your own power and authority. Ask yourself if you're playing too safe or are just being sensible. Try not to put barriers up – you don't want to live a half life emotionally in work – it's such a waste for you and your people"*

Work should be a place of enjoyment, excitement, inspiration and, yes, hard and productive work. We know that people feel more happy and motivated when they believe you believe in them and care about how they are progressing.

"In order to motivate your people effectively, you have to love them at least a little"

How close should I get?
(some points to consider)

- If you don't show your team that you care about them, you won't be credible when you try to motivate them
- You don't need to be aloof to show who the boss is
- You can have fun but state the ground rules *"when the chips are down..."*
- Set clear boundaries with your team in and out of work if it gives you comfort
- You don't have to be everyone's best friend
- You don't have to behave like "the manager" in all situations
- You can show emotion
- You can be you
- Your business decisions should never be based on friendship
- Your business decisions should always be grounded in logic and empathy
- If you want to have a beer with your people, have a beer. If you don't – don't
- If you do have a beer, enjoy it, have fun but don't go completely crazy (everything in moderation except moderation)

These are merely some views and thoughts for you to consider. What you do on this issue is entirely your call.

Just be true to yourself and try to accept that you don't need to be apart and aloof to command respect, loyalty and dedication from your people.

TOP TIPS for the Loving Principle

- Think about the motivational needs of the people in your team routinely
- Review the 4 components regularly
- Everyone has a need for shelter, safety, belonging, respect and self actualisation. Work on helping your people satisfy these needs and they will feel motivated
- The intensity of a person's motivation to do what you need depends on their belief that they will get what they need if they do what you need. Use this understanding to specifically target your efforts to motivate individuals in your team
- Use the carrot style as the norm (Theory Y)
- Love your people (just a little bit)
- Always be yourself
- Use "The Thought" when talking to team members
- Choose how you develop your work and social life and how close you get with your people. Make your own decisions on this

"People say that motivation doesn't last. Well, neither does bathing, that's why we recommend it daily"
(Zig Ziglar)

PEP 5

The Scoring Principle

ASSESSING PERFORMANCE

This is where we move into the area of formally assessing the performance of your people. Let's just remind ourselves where we've got to on managing performance so far:

- PEP 1 – Set clear objectives
- PEP 2 – Daily praising/challenging – informal
- PEP 3 – Monthly 1-1s – semi formal

PEP 5 is the climax of these connected principles. It's where, as a manager, you look back over the whole year and make an assessment of how well a person has performed.

Now, most organisations have a **process, documentation and a rating scale** for helping you do this. Some **organisations link the performance assessment to pay rises or bonuses**, but some do not. All performance assessments have an **impact on an individuals promotion prospects** though, so no matter what your organisation's approach, there really is plenty of skin in the game for you and your employees.

Organisations use different terminology to describe these highlighted areas but nearly all will recognise them as their "performance management processes". If you don't already know how these processes work in your business, you need to find out right away as this PEP will make much more sense if you first know how they operate in your own organisation.

This PEP will cover the issues you should consider when assessing performance together with some of the pitfalls you should seek to avoid. It will also cover some general tips for carrying out successful performance review discussions.

The 3 keys to reviewing and assessing performance

The great thing about reviewing performance is that, if you've followed the other PEPs, this becomes relatively easy. Three simple steps are involved:

1. Preparation and collection of feedback
2. Considering the performance rating
3. Carrying out the Performance Review discussion

Lets's take each one in turn

1) Preparation and Collection of Feedback

- ❑ Look over the 1-1 and general notes you've made through the year in the individual's performance file (See PEPs 1, 2 and 3)
- ❑ Review what's been achieved against each performance objective agreed through PEP 1
- ❑ Take feedback from colleagues and customers on how the individual has performed.

Covering these areas will provide you with a very rounded view of the individual's performance over the year.

As part of the preparation you should strongly encourage your team member to undertake similar preparation for the review so that you have a good basis for discussion.

2) Considering the Performance Rating

Organisation etiquette for rating decisions can vary so it's always worth checking if your organisation has any specific approaches or rules to rating performance.

Your rating or assessment should be a broad summary of the 1-1s you've had throughout the year. By undertaking the preparation outlined earlier you will have developed a very rich picture on which to make your rating decision

Here are a few traps to avoid when making your decision:

Surprise – there should be no bad surprises for any individual. Monthly 1-1s are the place to voice any performance concerns you've had previously. Don't spring a bad surprise, they should already know how you are viewing their performance. Clearly, some people will be in denial and you won't be able to account for that but be sure to have been honest through the year not just at the annual performance review.

Horns and halo – Avoid the blue eyed boy or girl syndrome or writing someone off. Rarely is someone's performance all good or all bad. Look at your evidence thoroughly and be fair with your conclusion.

Recency – Review the whole year, don't be overly swayed by performance delivered in the last few months

Personality Driven – if you have stronger personal connections with some of your team, avoid showing favouritism in your decision making just because you like them

Inconsistency – Consider your performance ratings when you are feeling relaxed and in control of your emotions. Making decisions when feeling elated or depressed or angry is not the best basis for demonstrating balance and fairness in your performance ratings. Also, try to make your rating decisions in the same "session" so that you can compare and contrast performance of different individuals unhindered by being in different moods on different days.

What rating to give?

Organisation's performance rating scales vary but the majority work using one of the following approaches.

- Even scales – Performance assessed out of 4, 6 or 8
- Odd scales – Performance assessed out of 3, 5 or 7

A typical 5 rating scale would look something like that illustrated below

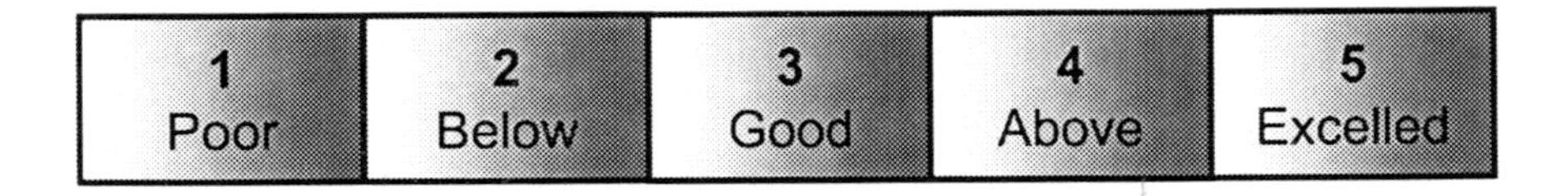

Your organisation may also impose or recommend a distribution for these ratings.

5% Poor	15% Below	60% Good	15% Above	5% Excelled

I personally favour odd numbered scales where there is an exact mid point. This allows you to clearly show that you are rating an individual as doing a good job in meeting the objectives without having to force you into a decision on whether they are above or below the requirements of the role which is driven when you have an even numbered scale.

Not everyone shares this view and even numbered scales can work effectively. I just have a particular aversion to a system that doesn't provide a natural "rating" for the vast majority of the workforce who do the job you need them to do – no more, no less.

You'll need to work with whatever guidelines and processes operate in your business but all the tips here should apply no matter what the make up of your performance management system is.

When rating individuals, it's easy to make your decision on the clear overachievers and the poor performers. The decision gets harder when you think the individual's performance is on the "cusp" of the next rating, lower or higher.

A useful "trick" I've used to help my decisions on this is to write out your team sheet. Imagine you're picking your football or hockey team. Best players first, worst players last. Write out your team sheet

Peggy
John
David
Peter
Seth
Amanda
Emma
Clinton

Andrew
Deborah
Jude
Robert

Seeing your team like this makes it easier to think about where you will draw in the lines of the different performance ratings. You can play around with different places for the line until you are satisfied you have it right.

Peggy John	***Excelled***
David	***Above***
Peter Seth Amanda Emma Clinton Andrew Deborah	***Good***
Jude	***Below***
Robert	***Poor***

Although this may seem hugely simplistic, I've genuinely found it remarkably effective in deciding where to draw the line. Very importantly, this list should not be shared with your team, it is purely an aid to your decision process.

3) Carrying out the Performance Review Discussion

If you have followed the Milestone principle effectively, carrying out this final performance review is little more than a final 1-1 discussion summarising the previous 1-1s.

Yes, you will also confirm the performance rating and firm up on development plans but the "ease" of this discussion is driven by how well you've carried out your monthly 1-1s.

So let's just summarise the approach:

- **Before the Discussion**
  - Follow the Milestone principle throughout the year
  - Make your rating decision
  - Be aware that you may have missed something and be prepared to adjust your performance notes and even the rating decision
  - Book sufficient time for the review (1-2 hours)
  - Make sure you have sufficient privacy for the discussion and ensure you won't be interrupted
- **During the Discussion**
  - Remember it's **their** review so try to get them to do most of the talking (you have two ears and one mouth, try to use them in that proportion in this discussion)
  - Review performance against all key objectives (their view and your view)

- o Look out for development opportunities (More on this in PEP 6)
- o Praise where relevant
- o Be clear, firm but nurturing on areas where performance hasn't met the objectives you've agreed (from PEP 1).

❑ **After the Discussion**

- o Simply make sure all the paperwork is completed and any agreed actions are carried out. Believe me, people get quickly cheesed off when they have a good appraisal discussion with their boss and no formal confirmation follows.

❑ **Having an Argument**

Frankly, no matter how well you prepare for the performance review discussion and how clear you are in your monthly 1-1s, you will occasionally come across an individual who just doesn't accept your performance rating.

Clearly, the chances of avoiding this situation are greatly increased if you follow the PEPs you've read about so far but, I guarantee, you will come across this situation on many occasions in your management career.

You see, whilst many people have a capacity for demonstrating humility, most have a tendency to believe that they're really good at what they do or that other people/things get in the way of them being really good. One of the psychological terms for this is "Denial".

So, here are some helpful hints should this situation occur:

- Stay calm, ask them why they think their rating should be different
- Listen but restate your own case calmly
- Refer them to previous feedback
- Stay assertive – don't be bullied
- Be honest
- If you think they've got a point, you may wish to get more details and say you'll think about it and come back to them tomorrow.
- If the individual gets overly emotional, end the discussion at that moment and rebook for later that day or the following day.

So that's it, a whistle stop tour of how you go about reviewing and assessing performance. I'm sure you're starting to see how each PEP builds to another and makes later PEPs easier to deliver.

SIMPLE ??

EUREKA !!!

TOP TIPS for the Scoring Principle

- First deliver PEPS 1,2,3 – they are immensely helpful to you in delivering this principle
- Find out how "performance management" works in your business
- Collect feedback and prepare thoroughly before you assess performance
- Avoid the traps of assessment (horns/halo, recency, personality driven, inconsistency)
- If you are having difficulty making your rating decisions, try the "team sheet" method for assessing individual performance in your team
- Use the hints list for carrying out the performance review discussion
- Stay calm if your team member wants to argue the performance rating
- Do it your own way, but do do it

"Lack of opportunity is often nothing more than a lack of purpose or direction" (anon)

PEP 6

The Growing Principle

DEVELOPING YOUR PEOPLE

"If we did all the things we are capable of doing , we would literally astound ourselves" (Thomas Edison)

Growing and developing your team members to perform their role better is one of your key responsibilities as a manager.

Of course, individuals are responsible for their own development but this principle is about the things you need to do to create the right environment of support to help them become the performers they can be.

WHY SHOULD YOU PROVIDE SUPPORT?

A lot of managers ask this question especially when they are under workload pressure and developing their people seems to fall lower and lower down the priority list.

Let me give you 5 simple reasons why you should always keep developing your people as a high priority:

1. They get the job done better if they receive the right development support.

2. Your job gets easier as you end up having to sort out fewer problems.

3. Your business benefits from improved employee performance now and from a developing pool of talent for the future.

4. The individual benefits by developing new skills and we know that development itself is motivational to most people.

5. You will need to continue developing your people to keep pace with ever increasing business demands and to replace team members who occasionally move on from your team.

Breaking the Cycle

Despite the obvious benefits, it's so easy to forget about development when you're under pressure. It's ironic that most managers come under personal work pressure as a result of their people not knowing enough, not being fast enough or not being motivated enough to deliver what they are capable of.

A vicious cycle is created where you haven't enough time to develop your people because you end up doing work which they could do if you were able to develop them.

So, **break the cycle** and always keep development high on your priority list and turn it into a virtuous cycle. You spend time developing your people, helping them become more able to perform. This reduces work pressure on you which then allows you more time to focus on their development.

Simple to say, hard to do!! I agree, but if **you** don't do it, who will??

SO WHAT "DEVELOPMENT" ARE WE TALKING ABOUT HERE?

Well, the things you will be looking for the person to develop or adapt will usually fall into one of the following categories:

- **Knowledge** –What an individual needs to know to perform their role effectively (e.g. processes, products, systems, targets and standards).
- **Skills** – How well an individual applies the knowledge in the performance of their role (e.g. selling skills, building skills, negotiation, influence, customer service etc).
- **Attitude and behaviour** – How well an individual demonstrates the behaviour appropriate for the role (e.g. politeness, motivation, punctuality, care, conscientiousness etc).

These are the three development areas you should always consider when talking about development in your monthly 1-1s and annual performance reviews. It's also part of your Daily Principle too in the "praising and challenging" and "sharing and guiding" activities.

HOW TO HELP YOUR PEOPLE DEVELOP

There are a few simple steps when considering and discussing development with your people:

- Step 1 – Spot the development need
- Step 2 – Help identify the possible development solution
- Step 3 – Make sure solution gets delivered
- Step 4 – Check whether the improvement you wanted has happened

Let's take each one in turn:

Step 1 – Spot the development need

We've pretty much covered this already. Keep an eye out for potential gaps in knowledge, skills, attitude and behaviour, discuss what you see with the individual and ask their opinion, you may have missed something. It's really important that this is a two way conversation.

Step 2 – Help identify the possible development solution

Discuss with your team member how they would like to be helped. There are many varied options available in all businesses to develop people. If you have a learning and development team within your HR department, use them to get advice on what's available for your people. There's plenty you can initiate within your own department though.

Here's some examples of possible learning options for you to consider

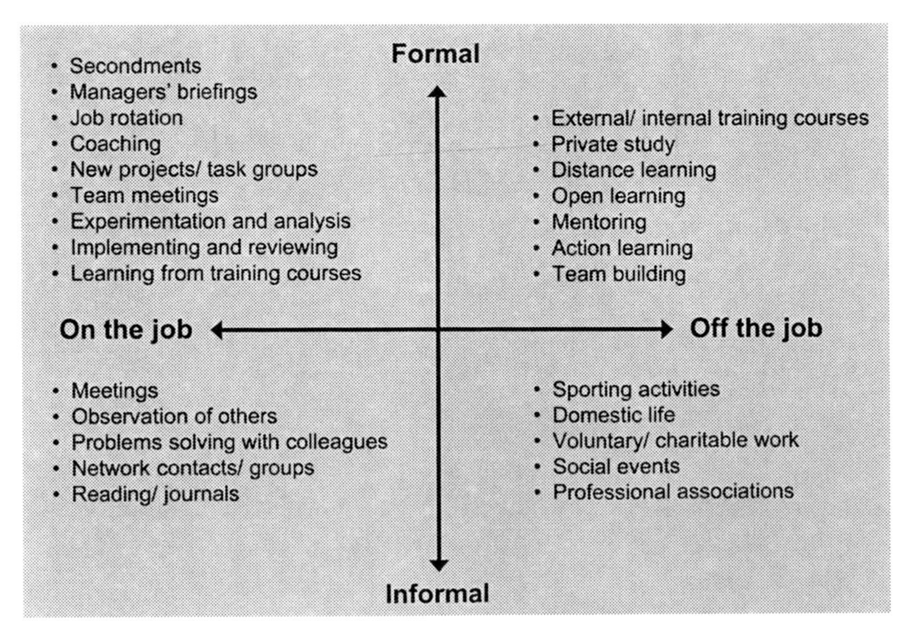

The key thing is to agree with your team member that the development need is real and relevant. Then agree which solution would be most appropriate for them in the circumstances. Be sensitive to the fact that what has worked for you in the past might not necessarily work well for them. Open discussion is important here.

STEP 3 – MAKE SURE THE SOLUTION GETS DELIVERED

This step is really simple. Make sure the individual takes ownership for ensuring the development takes place. Keep it on your 1-1 agenda until all steps are completed.

If you are part of the solution (e.g. you've agreed to provide the individual with personal coaching on a particular development area), make sure you deliver on what you've promised.

STEP 4 – CHECK WHETHER THE IMPROVEMENT YOU WANTED HAS HAPPENED

Once the solution has been delivered, review with the individual how well he or she believes it has helped. Then keep an eye out for examples of improvement and keep it on your 1-1 agenda to discuss until you're satisfied that the development need has been resolved. You may decide a further solution may be appropriate from time to time where the required progress hasn't been achieved.

Oh, and don't forget to maintain records on the performance file throughout.

Final Thought

Whilst the theory of learning is a very wide ranging subject and easily capable of filling a book in itself, following the simple steps and Top Tips of this PEP consistently will set you apart from most managers.

Start doing these things now and, over time, take the opportunity to develop your own knowledge around the theory of learning – there are plenty of really good books out there.

"The whole purpose of learning is to be able to see, do or consider something in a different way. We have to learn in order to develop ourselves as people"

TOP TIPS – The Growing Principle

- Remind your people that they are responsible for their own development but you are there to support and guide them
- Think about development in terms of knowledge, skills and attitude or behaviour
- Talk about development with each team member at their monthly 1-1s, annual performance reviews and as part of your Daily Principle actions
- Discussions should be two way. You want your team member's view on their development needs too
- Use the 4 step process:
    1. Spot the development need
    2. Help identify the possible development solution (Use the Learning Options Grid)
    3. Make sure solution gets delivered
    4. Check whether the improvement you wanted has happened
- Break the cycle – find the time to develop your people!
- Use the 4 step process to develop people for the future by using Step 1 to consider the development needs for their next job rather than just their current job

- As part of your own development, consider whether you'd like to find out more about the theory of learning in the future and put it in your own development plan

"Learning is not compulsory, but neither is survival"
(W. Edwards Deming)

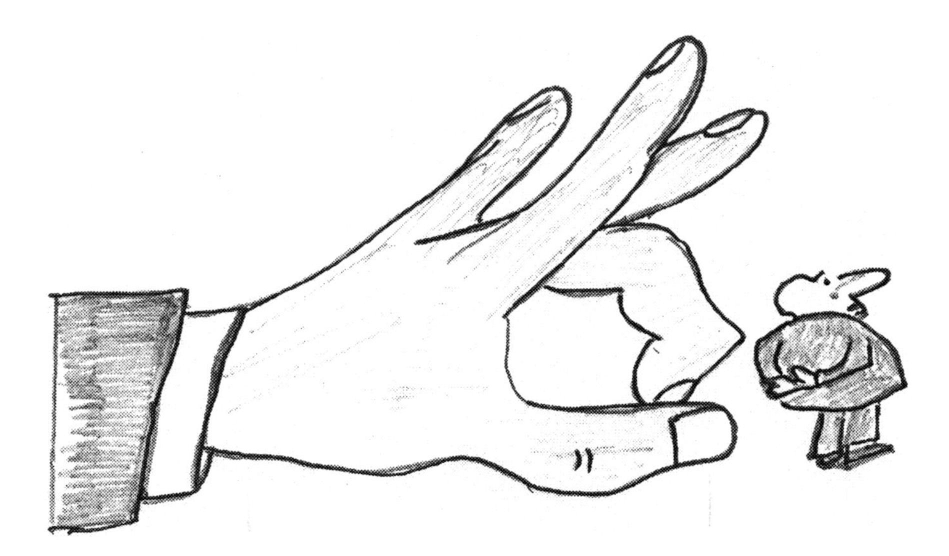

PEP 7

The Sacking Principle

DEALING WITH UNDER-PERFORMANCE

Sometimes, no matter how well you follow the other principles, you may find a member of your team is consistently not responding to your performance requirements.

This comes in various guises - underperformance against targets, undermining you or others in the team, upsetting customers and colleagues with their behaviour, not following processes etc.

Let's be very simple and clear about this. If you are consistently applying the earlier PEPs and an individual is not responding you have three options:

1) Ignore it, hope it goes away and the individual gets with your programme.
2) Ship the problem to someone else.
3) Solve the problem and exit the individual from your team and the business.

Ignore underperformance at your peril. If you don't deal with performance issues you lose credibility with your other team members and your peers. In a business sense this is a kill or be killed situation.

My plea, as a fellow manager, is don't ship the problem. In my experience, the reason that we all know at least one breath-takingly inept senior manager whatever business we work in is because other managers have continually shipped the problem over the years. Too many business disasters occur further down the line. You are delaying the inevitable exit and getting another manager to pick up **your** problem.

So, solve the problem - draw the line in the sand and say to yourself...

..."the buck stops here".

But Can't They Be Saved?

Absolutely, the shock of a boss being very clear, direct and explicit about their performance shortfalls may well "shock" an individual into improved performance. I've seen it happen on rare occasions and, even then, nearly always when an individual has never previously received direct and explicit feedback.

So consider this principle as your last resort because the other PEPs aren't creating the response you need. You will have already set clear direction, provided regular feedback on performance, helped develop the individual's skills and helped create a motivational environment.

This PEP is about how you should go about solving the problem by exiting the individual from the business and, most importantly, keeping you lawful and ethical in the way that you do it.

Your conscience should remain clear throughout this process as you will see it is designed to give the individual lots of opportunity to put things right before you are forced to take the final steps to exit.

There are some very simple rules to follow in this process and this PEP chapter will be relatively short. The key thing is to follow ALL the rules.

"The time is always right to do what is right"
(Martin Luther King)

OK, before we start with the rules, when is the right time to start the process of exiting someone rather than just "challenging" and developing them?

Whenever I'm talking to managers about Performance Management, this is the question I get asked more than any other. The simple answer is that it's always the right time as your actions are no more than an extreme route taken on the continuous process of performance management.

This isn't as complicated as it sounds. You're already doing most of the steps through the other PEPs. Let me show you the process….

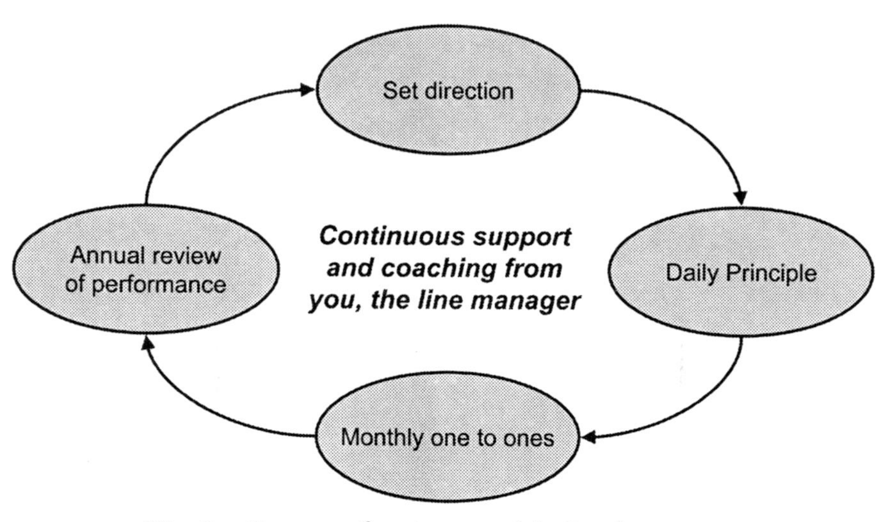

Fig 8 - Process for Acceptable Performance

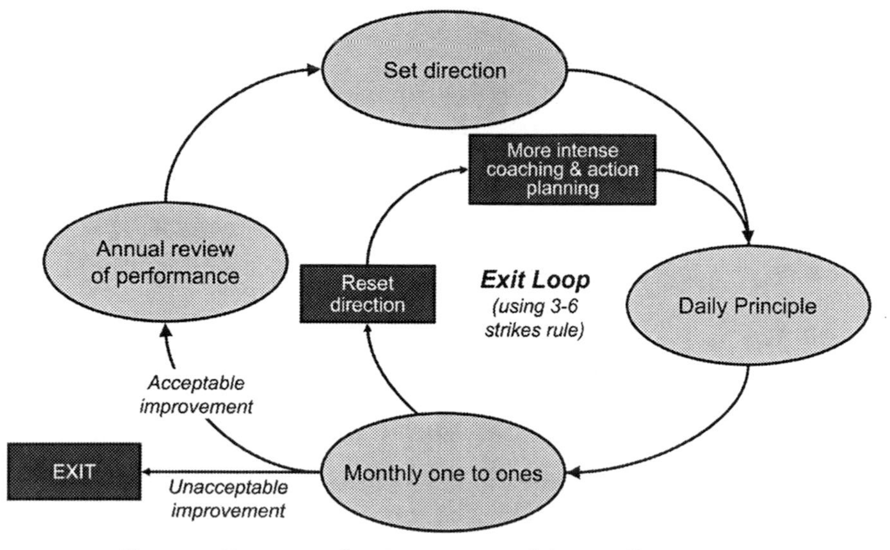

Fig 9 - Process for Unacceptable Performance

The Acceptable Performance process in figure 8 is a representation of what you're doing following the other PEPs concerned with managing performance.

The Unacceptable Performance process in figure 9 just has an extra loop added to it which I call the Exit Loop.

The Exit Loop.

The only difference in your approach at the beginning of an under-performance situation starts **after** you've given performance feedback in your monthly 1-1.

From here, you should re-clarify the performance objectives to ensure the individual understands what is expected of them. Then provide more intensive coaching support to help them improve their performance related to the problems you have raised. It's also sensible to increase the frequency of your 1-1s at this point to provide time for the increased coaching and to discuss whether the improvement you need is happening.

Rules for Exiting.

1) Record keeping - Recording clear and complete notes* of your 1-1 discussions in the performance file is critical from now on as the notes will become very important later in the process of exiting. (* dates, actions agreed, conversations, feedback etc.)

2) 3-6 Strike Rule - This is just an indication of timescale. If performance hasn't improved to a level you are satisfied with in a 3-6 months timeframe, you should start involving your Human Resources department to assist you in the legalities of exiting the individual.

3) Keep your line manager informed from the beginning– you will need his or her support with HR to make this happen.

The remaining rules reflect what you'll usually need to do to get the support of your HR dept.

4) Show how you've set clear objectives

5) Show evidence of the clear feedback you've given the individual

6) Show evidence of under-performance since the issue became apparent

7) Show evidence of re-clarifying objectives

8) Show the support the individual has received from you and others.

9) Show how performance levels are still unacceptable

You can see why your performance file is essential here.

In most situations, you'll know by the 3rd month whether the individual will make the improvement you need or not.

Once you think the problem is likely to need resolving by exit you may decide to further increase the frequency of 1-1s, remembering to record fully all conversations you are having with the individual and the support you are making available.

This is also the time to first approach your HR department for further guidance and support.

By following these simple rules, you can be sure that:

- you've done everything you can to help the individual improve.
- you will gain HR department support by involving them early in the process.
- you will have kept your company and yourself lawful doing the right things and having documentary evidence to prove this.
- you will gain credibility with your team, your peers and your boss by being seen to deal with under-performance effectively (a rare quality in managers).

One Final Thought

Folks, I know this is one of the hardest things we have to do as managers and, hopefully, it will only happen a few times in your whole career.

As well as the process being tough for the individual, it will be emotionally tough for you too. Make sure you talk to your HR department as well as your line manager so that you get the support you need in working through the situation.

By sticking to the process and taking advice from the right people, when it does happen, you'll be ready.

To be a great people manager you have to bite the bullet from time to time. Be courageous.

TOP TIPS for the Sacking Principle

- Deal with the problem, don't ship it
- When you start observing an unacceptable performance issue, bolt on the exit loop in your performance management process
- Follow PEPs 1,2,3 and 6, they are vital
- Keep detailed records on the performance file
- Keep your line manager updated from the beginning
- Use the 3-6 Strikes rule, don't delay the decision to involve HR if you know that performance isn't improving
- Involve HR early (and take advice)
- Be courageous

"Courage is not the absence of fear, but rather the judgement that something else is more important than fear"
(Ambrose Redmoon)

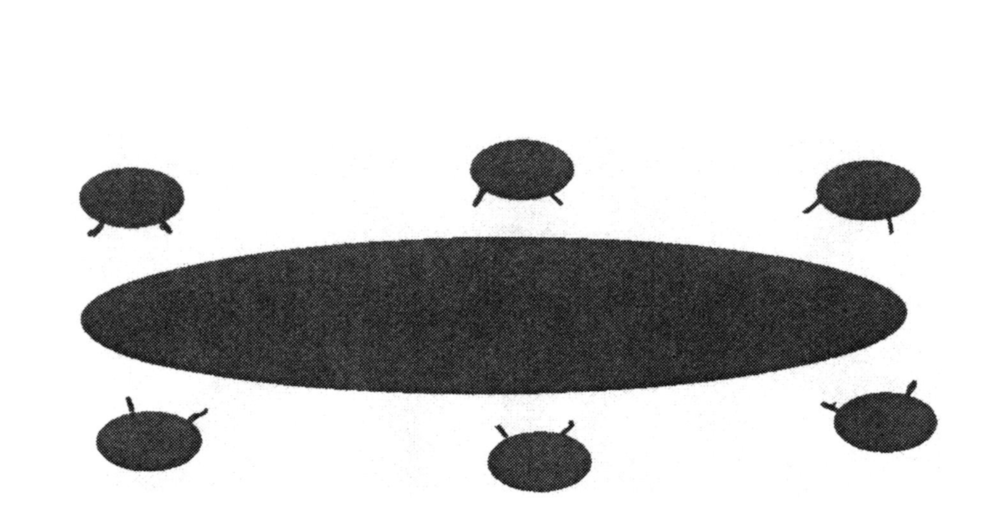

PEP 8

The Virtuous Principle

"BUILDING A TEAM"

"Individuals play the game but teams win championships" (anon)

So far, we've mainly concentrated on one on one interactions between you and your people in order that you can get the best out of them individually.

This PEP looks at how you can create a situation where ***"the whole is greater than the sum of the parts".***

Please don't groan. I know it's an old cliché but it hits the nail on the head ok!

This means creating an environment where, ***by working together, your people start delivering things for you and your customers that they just couldn't make happen individually.***

SO HOW DO YOU DO THIS?

Well, I guess the first thing to say is that it's a lot easier to talk about than do. You'll hear a lot of managers talk about *the need to create a team ethic*, or *the concept of team* or *the need to work together effectively* but few would be able to tell you what it really takes to create a strong team.

Let's start with some simple psychology.

You'll recall from PEP4 (The Loving Principle), that all people have a need to feel a sense of belonging. In the work context, this means they need to feel part of a group, most often a team.

Now this is great, because we're already half way there. They want it, we obviously want it…

…so what's the problem?

The problem isn't that they want it. It's that they want it under certain conditions.

Let's imagine we can hear what a team member is saying and thinking about the department.

(Says) "We need to work together more and support each other, we need to create a real team spirit here. It will be better for us and the customers!!"

(Thinks) "We need all of this, subject to:

1. The manager sees me as one of the best or the best performer in the team.
2. That Jackie stops bitching about me behind my back.
3. That Fred starts being nice to me and stops ignoring me.
4. That the manager deals with Harry who is the laziest so and so in the department.
5. That I don't have to work with Gemma.
6. That I can continue to work with John.
7. That the boss stops seeing Fred as the blue eyed boy".

I'm sure you get the drift. People have doubts, fears, aspirations and desires that can **limit** their motivation to work together collaboratively.

As their manager, you're the person who has the job of taking away as many of these limiting factors as reasonably possible so that your group of individuals can grow into a team.

If it's that complicated – why bother?

If you get it right, the benefits can be enormous. Better ideas, problems being resolved before you're even aware there's an issue, happy and motivated people who support and develop each other without realising it, culminating in a much better service for your customers and more time for you to manage effectively.

In short, great teams always create a great place to work and deliver great service!

"Team work is the fuel that allows ordinary people to attain extra-ordinary results"

More good news!

Although removing the limiting factors sounds complicated, the good news is that you're already doing most of the things you need to do to create a successful team by following the PEPs you've already read about.

Here are some simple steps to develop your team that will build on the good work you're already doing with each individual.

1) Create a shared sense of purpose

Be clear with your team about the vision you have for your department. Share with them the picture of what you want the department to become, what people and customers will say about it, what you want it to feel like to work there. Make the vision compelling, stretching but realistic. Show them how excited you are by it.

This is about creating a broad sense of direction for everyone that works for you and as a result, is most effectively communicated to groups of people rather than 1 on 1. Involve them with questions like "if you like this vision, what do we need to do together to help make it happen?"

"Vision is describing what life could be like while dealing with life as it is"(anon)

2) Put "team-working" on everyone's performance objectives

Remember setting individual performance objectives with each team member in performing PEP 1?

Well, "team-working" should now be added to the list of objectives for each individual. The measure ("evidenced by") can be a combination of your observation and feedback gained from the other team members the individual is working with.

3) Create shared objectives

Where you think it's appropriate, create common objectives between some team members through PEP1. This could be on a joint project where work has to be done together or a process where work is handed over at certain points. Just be clear on who is leading the activity to avoid any power struggles.

So, points 2 and 3 ensure there is reward and consequence for each individual in terms of how well they work for the team. In other words, a team working objective means individuals have "skin in the game" as this will have some impact on their annual performance rating (PEP 5).

4) Praise and Challenge team behaviour

We've covered this in PEP2 so you're probably **already** getting some "praising and challenging" practice.

As part of this, make sure you consistently **praise good team behaviour** and reprimand bad behaviour. Once your people know you're serious about creating good team interactions they'll start displaying the behaviours you are looking for.

"On this team, we're all united in a common objective: to keep my job!" (Lou Holtz - US Football coach 1937)

5) Show trust in your people, empower them

It would be hard for the team members to work together effectively if you are checking their work every minute. Show trust in them to come up with ideas in groups and to implement them. You will always have to balance the risk of you stepping back with the benefits of giving them space to work together and develop their relationships.

You want controlled empowerment not uncontrolled chaos so you should ensure they come to you to with an idea and the solution before they start implementing something new. Just make sure you look for the positives and be encouraging wher-ever possible. (PEPs 4 and 6)

Understanding how to empower your people is a very popu-lar and interesting managerial subject, and a useful managerial skill. I recommend you add this subject to your future reading list as part of your own development plan.

6) Fairness and Equity

For long term team success, it's important that you demon-strate fairness in the decisions and assessments you make and show equity in the opportunities you afford people.

It's worth noting that favouritism can be perceived in many forms, from you providing better opportunities to some, to you avoiding "challenging" those who deserve it where they are seen by others to be "getting away with it".

Sometimes, you will make decisions to give more opportunity to your best performers or more experienced people - and that's fine - you have a rationale which can be communicated to the team. Even if some don't like the decision, they can't argue with the logic.

Being human, you will always have people in your team you naturally like more than others. The key thing is to avoid any sort of favouritism based on these personal likes or dislikes.

In PEPs 2 and 4 we discussed how all team members think it's important to feel they are treated fairly. They will quickly point fingers and blame you if they feel others are receiving more favourable treatment than them.

A lack of fair treatment will undermine your team members' desire to work collaboratively with those they think are getting more favourable treatment. This acts as a real blocker to developing a team where some are seen as *"more equal than others"*. It creates a *"them and us"* situation which can quickly descend into internal war games where everyone, but particularly you and your customers, loses.

FINAL THOUGHT

So, creating a team isn't easy – you've got to want it bad because your people are going to put up a fight. This doesn't mean they don't want to work together, but more that they want "a team" under certain conditions. Some of these conditions are rational, some are not. Your role is to create an environment where all "reasonable" barriers are removed so that "the team" can be allowed to grow.

If you do this, the benefits can be immense, both personally and professionally. Being part of a great team creates a **virtuous cycle** where people help each other more, learn more, are more motivated and enthusiastic. This, in turn, feeds their desire and ability to help customers and team members even more effectively… and then the virtuous cycle continues and grows.

The "team" situation you have created will be noticed by others and they will want to work in your team. Other managers will notice this and you will start being seen as someone people want to work for. This is one of the ways we describe a true Leader!

I think this is something worth fighting for.
What do you think?

TOP TIPS for the Virtuous Principle

- Create a compelling vision for the team. Talk passionately to them about the type of behaviour you expect to see and what it will be like to be part of the team
- Put a "team–working" objective in everyone's Performance Objectives – this puts their "skin in the game"
- Praise good team behaviour and Challenge bad team behaviour – this shows your team it's important to you
- Encourage your people to work together on daily issues, empower them and back off
- It's not good enough to be fair and equitable, you have to **be seen** to be fair and equitable by your team
- Deal with underperformance as it can be seen as a form of favouritism if you don't
- Even though your people might put up a fight, never forget they want to work in a great team and you want the benefits of the virtuous cycle a team creates

"Coming together is a beginning, staying together is progress, but Working Together is Success!!"
(Henry Ford)

PEP 9

The Balancing Principle

"GETTING A LIFE"

By now, I'm sure you understand that PEPs 1-8 are interconnected in all sorts of very interesting ways. Delivering some of these PEPs helps you to deliver others.

That's pretty cool because, without seeing these interconnections, it would be easy to fall into the trap of viewing what we've already covered as 8 separate lists of "management stuff" you need to do. And the lists continue to grow don't they ???!!!

FEAR NOT!

Whilst we both know there is a fair bit to think about from the first eight PEPs, the good news is that the final two PEPs concentrate on helping you manage yourself in the delivery of the principles we've already covered.

In other words, the final PEPs are pretty much about helping you deal with the steps from the previous sections in this book.

In PEP 9, we'll focus on the critical component of finding some "balance" between your work as a manager and the other things you need beyond work in order to live a full and rich life.

WHAT'S THIS GOT TO DO WITH ME MANAGING OTHERS?

Good question, I'm glad you thought of it!! - Here's the deal. You're going to have to be on good form consistently to act really effectively as a manager. A theme running through the PEPs has been the need to act consistently with your people. To do this, you need a solid foundation to support you in the delivery of your managerial responsibilities.

Most days, you need to feel well rested, healthy, attentive, calm and ideally happy in order to deliver the right level of attention and response when your people interact with you.

"Work, work, work does not work for great managers, work, play, work does!!"

Over the years, there's been plenty of research published confirming that people, including managers, are more productive and make better decisions if they create "own-time" in their lives and don't overwork themselves. I'm not going to labour this point, let's just say that to stay fresh and sane as a manager...

..."you've gotta get a life man"(anon.)

I hear lots of managers who say things like, *I'll rest when I retire* or, *that's what the weekends are for.* This brand of hero management is heartening when looked at from the perspective of managers who demonstrate great belief and determination in what they are doing.

Unfortunately, it is immensely disheartening if you consider the life opportunities that can be missed when an extreme version of this approach is followed.

We all like to think we will do all the things we want to do before we die. But folks, it just isn't as simple as that. You have to make efforts to get a life, you even have to plan for it.

Why?

Because you haven't got as much time as you think!

Let's find out with a bit of math over the page.

Hurry!

The Scary "Own –Time" Calculation

If we assume a retirement age of 65, the following questions will show you the number of days of "own-time you have left until you retire.

Subtract your age from 65 ....

Multiply by 52 to get the number of weeks ________ **(A)**

Less:-

33% (of A) for work and commuting ....

33% for sleeping ....

8% for cooking, eating ....

4% for cleaning/tidying the house ....

2% for gardening ....

2% for washing clothes/ironing ....

1% for grocery shopping ....

Sub Total B ____________ **(B)**

Take away B from A to give you the total number of weeks you have left to do what you want to do until you are 65.

Total number of weeks left to do the things I want to do before I'm 65

.................weeks

Multiply this number by 7 for the total days – this often puts it into greater focus.

...................days

That's all you've got left!!

Told you it was scary!!

So, your "own time" is a really scarce resource. You should use it wisely to get as great a sense of personal balance and contentment as you can.

How well you spend your "own-time" is the foundation to prepare you for your work life. Good foundations from well spent "own-time" act as a primary source of the fuel or energy you need to perform your managerial role.

So, how do I spend my own time effectively?

Another good question! – You're on a roll !

The full answer is it depends on your circumstances. You will have some work and life things that are more important to you than others. There's plenty of written material in the market about how to live your life more effectively and, if you feel the need, go and look for more information after you've finished this book.

But, as you'd expect, I'm not going to leave you hanging on this one. Let me provide you with some common themes picked up from managers over the years. I'm sure most, if not all, will resonate with you.

5 areas to immediately consider for creating "balance"

1. Children and Partners
2. Wider Family and Friends
3. Time Poor but Cash Rich?
4. Working Late
5. Spoiling yourself

1) Children and Partners – The 30 minute thing

The Kids

If you have kids, make sure you get at least 30 minutes every week-day when they have your undivided attention in a positive, supportive or playful way. Undivided attention does not mean just being in the same room as them while you're watching the TV or typing your last few emails. It means having a conversation, a bit of fun or a game or just a cuddle with them. You know - when you are truly "with each other".

Kids love routine. It gives them comfort and a sense of stability and order. Try to do the 30 minute thing at the same time every day. If you're away on business or out with your friends, phone home and spend a few minutes with each of them knowing that tomorrow you'll be back in your routine.

Oh - by the way - Triple the timescale on weekends.

Only 90 minutes on weekends?

Doesn't seem that long does it. But just think - .How much "undivided attention" do you truly give your kids at the moment. Go on, think about it. You may be unpleasantly surprised.

If not, and you already do this then just keep doing what you're doing!!

Last word on kids. Get to school plays, sports days, parent-teacher conferences as often as you can. This is important to the kids and to your partner. You might not believe it now, but it's really important to you too.

So be the parent you can be as well as the leader and take some of my Mum's advice…

"You'll never get a second chance to do this stuff with your kids, they'll grow up before you realise so don't miss your chance"
(Nigel's Mum 1993)

Your partner

The importance of spending your "own time" with your partner is obvious I'm sure. I won't presume to suggest detailed approaches for this other than to say follow the same broad approach as with the kids. Clearly the content will be different but we all want some undivided attention so that we can satisfy our needs for love, laughter, support, feeling safe, wanted and respected.

Remember that when you give "undivided attention" you immediately receive it in return. So please don't regard this as a task, but more as a treat and a source of happiness for you and those you are closest to.

2) Wider Family and Friends

Spend time with the people you care about, don't lose touch. Choose to be happy and have fun. It's important to make the effort even when your initial instinct is to get an early night as it's all too easy to stop meeting your mates regularly because you're too tired or have too much work on.

It's ironic that the tiredness you're seeking to avoid by not meeting up can actually be cured by getting together. It can take your mind off work, give you a better sense of perspective, allow you to loosen up. In short, it can actually energise you.

"The time to relax is when you don't have time for it"
(Sidney Harris)

3) Time Poor but Cash Rich?

Generally speaking, I've found that the more senior a manager becomes, the longer hours s/he tends to work. As careers progress, work can increasingly impinge on weekends, bank holidays and even family holidays and special occasions.

Some of this impact can be softened by re-thinking your priorities as we've already covered, but the reality is that it can still be difficult to find all the time you need..

So, you're time poor but have plenty of money. Heard the expression, *lots of money but no time to spend it*? Here's two approaches that can help:-

Firstly, if you're in this situation, here's my phone number and bank account details, I'll be pleased to assist you on rebalancing the monetary side…

..**Sorry, couldn't resist**

Secondly, use some of your money to **buy your time back…..**

How to buy your time back

Simply make a list of all the things you spend time doing at the moment that eat into your "own-time". Then, pick out the items that you'd prefer not to do if you could get someone else to do them.

Here's some examples for you to consider:-

Cooking
Cleaning the house
Ironing clothes
Mowing the lawn
Painting and decorating
Grocery shopping
Washing the dishes
Washing clothes
Washing the car
Gardening
Other DIY
Ferrying the kids around

There will be businesses in your area for taking most burdens off your hands. They're equally adept at taking cash off your hands too so personal recommendations are always good to get before you buy.

Choose to "buy in" the tasks you really don't like doing or the most time consuming ones. Everyone's different so make your own personal choice. For example, I really dislike gardening but a friend of mine classes it as a hobby. Interestingly, his wife and kids all help out in the garden too. So, for them, gardening is a way for all the family to spend an enjoyable time together.

Being a kind soul, I offered him the opportunity to use my place as a further opportunity to spend time gardening with his family - but he rather impolitely declined. And there's me thinking I was going for a win:win scenario!!

I guess this is all a question of priorities. The strength of your desire to create time **versus** where you want and need to spend your money.

"Time is the most precious element of human existence"
(Denis Waitley)

4) Working Late

Working late is the key barrier in creating a good balance in your life. Quite simply, it robs you of "own-time" and so you need a strategy to minimise it.

Here are 3 simple rules for your consideration:-

- Leave work on time if you can. If you really have to do the work now, doing an extra hour at home is better for you and your family. Just you being present (even though working) can be comforting for you and them.
- If you have to stay late in the office, stay. Set a target time and when you leave, leave work thoughts behind completely.
- Never work on weekends* or holidays unless in an absolute emergency.

Keeping these rules will force others to be less reliant on you. If you find yourself always saying "Yes" to people's work requests, and working later and later you really should try following these rules or something similar that fits with your expected working pattern.*

The rules will force you to say "No" occasionally and, in doing so, this will educate others to be more realistic with work requests. It will also set a good example to your people as well as helping you avoid the dreaded burn–out situation.

"People who cannot find time for recreation are obliged sooner or later to find time for illness" (John Wanamaker)

"What is without periods of rest will not endure" (Ovid, Roman Poet)

5) Spoiling yourself

This is about being purely selfish and doing something that's just for you. Plan your commitments so that you make time to do whatever it is you love to do. This could be nurturing a hobby or interest, undertaking regular retail therapy, being pampered at a health club, doing lots of foreign travel….. Basically, whatever it is you want to do.

This sounds really neat I know. The key thing is to accept that all five areas need to be balanced with each other and alongside your work life.

That's a lot of Balancing!

Final Thoughts

Avoiding the trap of becoming a workaholic is a serious and sometimes difficult pursuit. A better balance in your life helps you be a better manager, a better friend, a better spouse, a better parent and, frankly, a more interesting person all round.

There has to be some planning in this because, if you really want balance, you will need to create a lifestyle where you deliver well for your employer and team and simultaneously ensure that your personal life is not compromised. You can't leave this to chance, and it won't just fall into a natural routine – you have to plan for it and work at it!

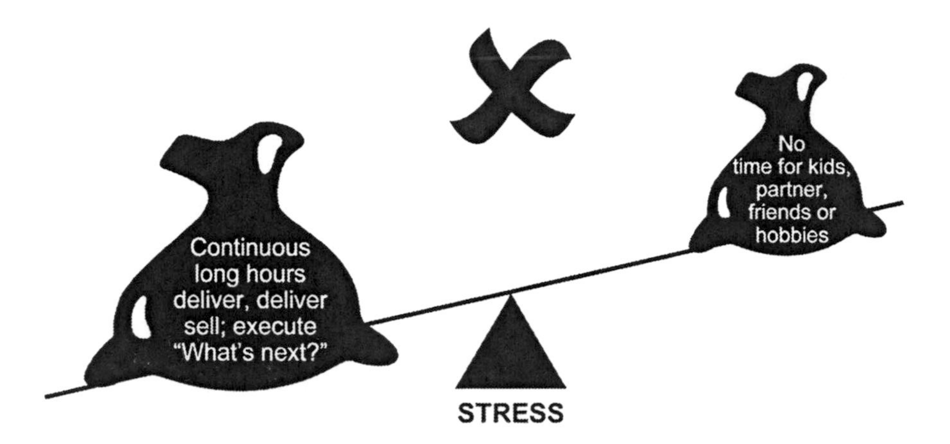
Continuous
long hours
deliver, deliver
sell; execute
"What's next?"
No
time for kids,
partner,
friends or
hobbies
STRESS

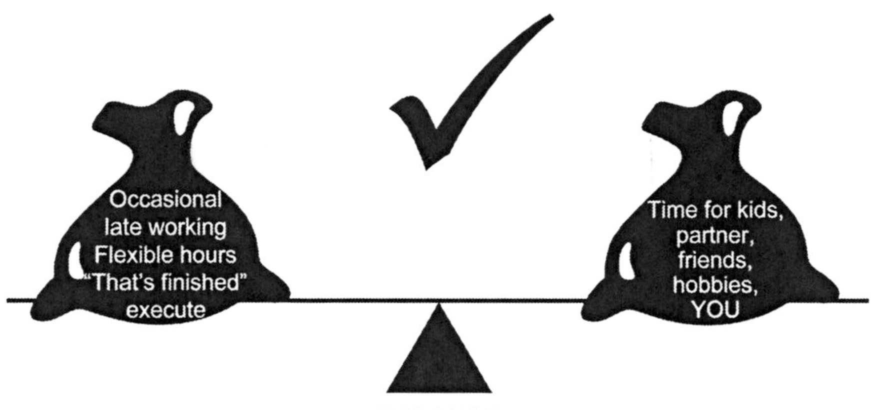
Occasional
late working
Flexible hours
"That's finished"
execute
Time for kids,
partner,
friends,
hobbies,
YOU
BALANCE

TOP TIPS for the Balancing Principle

- Creating a balance between work life and home life is essential to you being the manager you can be
- Accept that you don't need to be a "hero manager"
- Plan for making the most out of your "own time"
- Use the "**thirty minute thing**" with your children and your partner
- Make and keep regular commitments to your extended family and friends
- If you've got the money, buy the time
- Create your own rules for working late. Ensure the rules match to your "own-time" needs
- Spoil yourself regularly (and those closest to you)

"Happiness is a direction, not a place"
(Sydney Harris)

1.
2.
3.

PEP 10

The Execution Principle

"MAKING IT HAPPEN"

This final PEP is about how you put all the earlier stuff together so you can create a clear plan of action that you can "execute" in a way that is highly effective now and in the future.

In other words, ***"how to make it happen"!***

To do this really effectively, you'll need to follow just 3 simple but important steps:

1. Become a believer.
2. Choose to get motivated and excited about doing these things.
3. Create a clear plan of action and follow it!

Step 1 - Become a believer

If you believe most of the things you've read in each PEP make sense, will make you a better manager and can be realistically accomplished, then class yourself as a believer and move onto Step 2. You need to believe these things will make a difference and are worth pursuing if you are going to be motivated to execute the plan.

If you don't believe, try talking to other managers in your organisation (who you see as successful) and find out how they think they are successful. You'll see a lot of similarities, I'm sure.

If you're still unconvinced then ask yourself one final question

...So what's the alternative?

Step 2 - Choose to get motivated and excited

There's no getting away from the fact that you're going to come up against a few barriers and problems along your journey to follow the PEPs. To stay solid and remain firm in your convictions about what's important when others occasionally doubt or question you, or when you're under time or workload pressure requires a great deal of belief in what you are doing and a strong desire to get it done.

A useful way of helping yourself get motivated and remain motivated is to visualise how your team and you will be, when **you** are consistently following all the PEPs in an elegant way.

We covered something similar to this in PEP 8 (The Virtuous Principle) where you were getting your team motivated towards your "compelling team vision".

Personal Visioning – try this exercise when you have some privacy. It may help to close your eyes or focus on one spot on the wall as you follow the steps.

- Try to visualise how great your team and you will be when **you** are executing all the PEPs
- As you visualise...
    - ...add details like chairs desks, offices, posters
    - ...put colour into the image
    - ...now add sound
    - ...now make the picture move like a short movie
    - ...now make it great.
    - ...and notice how good you feel
- Keep replaying the short movie and try to hold onto the images and how great you are feeling.

You can use this vision to keep you motivated and to regularly remind you what you are aiming for. It will give you strength when setbacks occur.

Now that you believe what you are doing is the right course and feel really motivated towards getting there, you're ready to take the final step.

Step 3 - Create a clear plan of action and follow it!

When the idea of the PEPs came to me, I visualised them as bricks in a wall with one row acting as the foundation for the next. The pyramidal image on the front cover of this book is a simple way of demonstrating an overview of what's included in the PEPs.

However, for planning purposes, the pyramid diagram below is a more specific illustration of how I'd recommend you tackle your implemention.

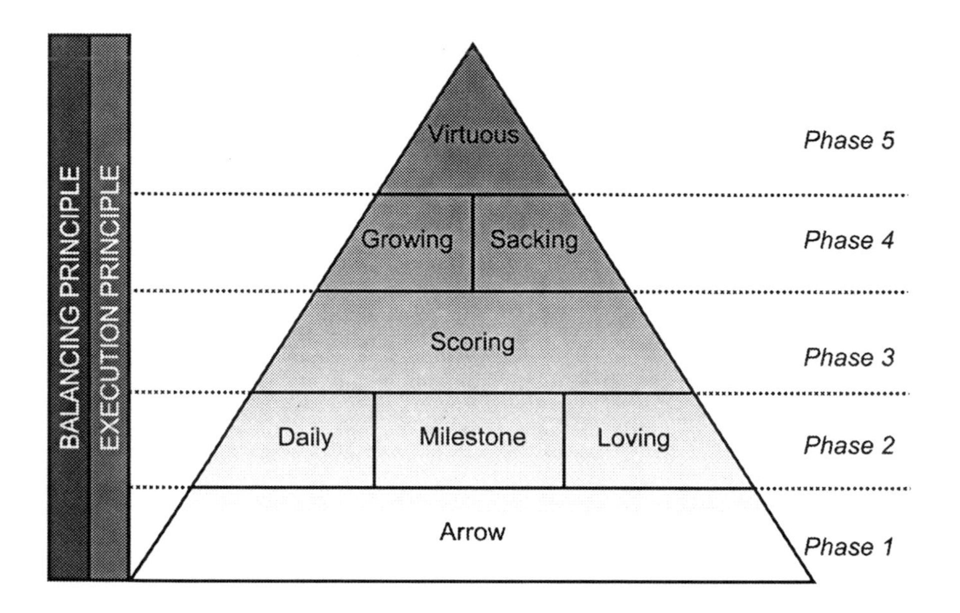

In designing this, I kept in mind that the key thing was to construct it in a way that allows you to take small steps. Small steps give you a better chance to sustain the changes you make and won't lead your team to think you've had one of those overnight "personality transplants" I keep mentioning.

"Nothing will lose you credibility with your people faster than having an overnight personality transplant"

Here's a quick reference guide to the illustration…

Phase 1

- **PEP** – Arrow Principle

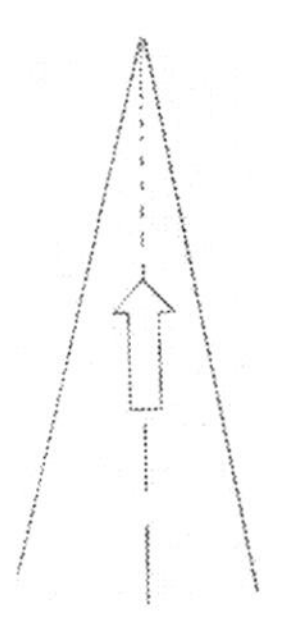

- **Why** – Start with being clear about everyone's objectives. Setting clear direction for all individuals has to be the first step on which to build everything else.
- **Recommended timescale** – First month (Agree all objectives and document in performance file)

Phase 2

- **PEPs** – Daily, Milestone, Loving Principles

- **Why** – These are inter-connected principles related to daily management, monthly 1-1s and motivational behaviour. They relate to the management actions you can start immediately after performance objectives have been agreed.
- **Recommended timescale** – Second month onward. These are now continuous activities so start with the basics and keep practicing and improving from one month to next.

Phase 3

- **PEP** – Scoring Principle

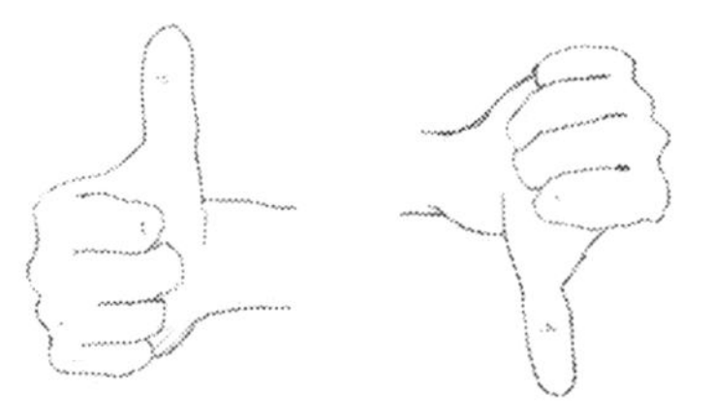

- **Why** – This is the annual or half yearly assessment of performance. It's the culmination of phase 2 activity. It is the planned opportunity for you to formally assess the quality of a persons performance.
- **Recommended Timescale** – Months 6 and 12 in your company's performance year

Phase 4

- **PEPs** – Growing, Sacking Principles

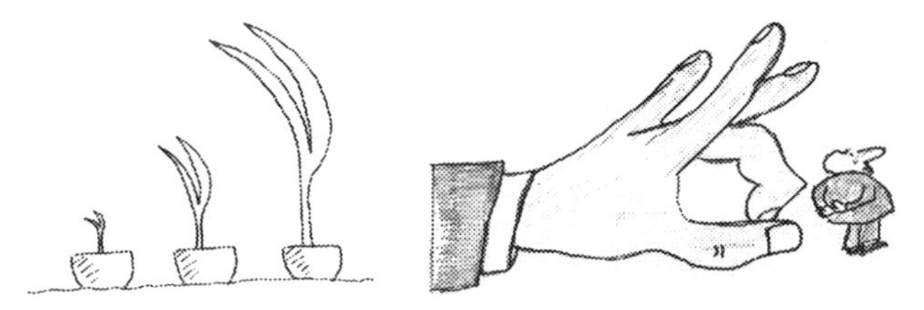

- **Why** – Some of this will come into your implementation of Phase 2 through your monthly 1-1s,. The activities for developing your people (Growing) or exiting them for under-performance (Sacking) will nearly always start as a result of formal performance appraisal (Scoring Principle).

- **Recommended Timescale** – This is an ongoing, continuous process but the cycle starts immediately after annual or half yearly performance review. So, in the first year, your effort should be formalised from Month 7 although you will informally start some of this as early as Phase 2 in your 1-1s.

PHASE 5

- **PEP** – Virtuous Principle

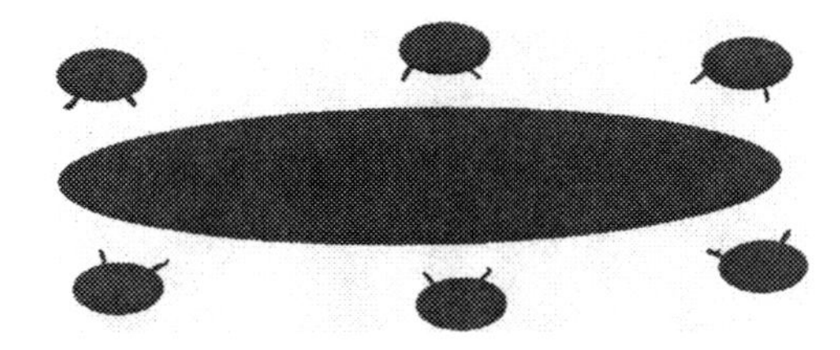

- **Why** – Left until last as you need to be effectively following the PEPs related to individuals before putting further time and effort into developing a real team ethic.

- **Recommended Timescale** – Start sometime in months 7 – 12. The key trigger is to start only when you are satisfied that you are consistently following at least the main points of the other PEPs.

The Other PEPs – Balancing and Execution

- **Why** – These are principles that support you to deliver your action plan so stand alongside the plan rather than part of it.

- **Recommended Timescale** - You will be following the Execution principle as soon as you start executing the action plan so this starts day 1. You have a high degree of freedom in choosing when to start implementing the Balancing Principle. You may find it harder in the first few months to create "own-time". However, as a general rule of thumb, this principle should be forming a key part of your general routine by month 7-12.

Final Thought

The plan I've recommended in this chapter is designed to give you a head start in the challenge of implementing the PEPs. You should decide whether the timescales are right for you and whether the order of implementation makes sense given the position you and your team are currently in. Make whatever changes you need. The important thing is to have a plan that works for you and your team, not anyone else.

You know, you could prepare the best plan in the world but if you don't possess the motivation and determination to follow it through, the plan will be nothing more than a waste of paper and a further contribution to global warming.

So, truly commit to the ideas you will use, truly commit to your plan and make sure your timescales are realistic before you start to implement this stuff. Let this is be your recipe for great execution.

"Quality is never an accident; it is always the result of high intention, sincere effort, intelligent direction and skilful execution. It represents the wise choice of many alternatives"

(William Foster)

TOP TIPS for the Execution Principle

- ❑ Only start executing an action plan if you believe in the PEPs you've read about
- ❑ Visualise to get excited and motivated about the implementation of the PEPs
- ❑ Prepare a clear plan of action that's right for your situation
- ❑ Consider how some PEPs need to be in place before other PEPs can be effectively implemented
- ❑ Take small steps rather than giant leaps
- ❑ Stay strong, stick with your plan when others might doubt you or you doubt yourself – perseverance will pay off
- ❑ Do it your own way, but do do it!

"It often requires more courage to dare to do right than to fear to do wrong" Abraham Lincoln

MY FINAL THOUGHTS

"I take the view and always have, that if you cannot say what you want to say in 20 minutes you ought to go away and write a book about it." Lord Brabazon (House of Lords 1955)

Well, I knew it might take longer than 20 minutes but I hope you've found the book short enough to stay interested and long enough to be useful !!

In any case, you've now read all but the final 2 pages. By now, you'll have become very comfortable with the Management PEPs and understand that much of each PEP is a large measure of common sense coupled with treating your people in a considerate, caring and "loving" way.

Hardly rocket science I know. However, you'll also now appreciate that the truly exceptional managers stand apart because they find a way of connecting the PEPs together so that one activity feeds into another or contributes to another.

Exceptional managers put the right processes in place and execute these processes with a great compassion for their people but in their own authentic style. That's why these have been underlying and repeating themes throughout this book.

The exceptional manager also delivers one final but vital ingredient. – **Consistency.** The execution of the PEPs for exceptional managers isn't just *"a bunch of things I have to do as part of the day job"*.

It **is** the day job!

"You are an individual and have the right to behave, manage and lead others as you see fit as long as it's lawful, ethical and respectful"

Great managers follow the PEPs consistently and continuously. It is the way they live their life. They are able to sustain this because they do it in their own unique style rather than wasting energy pretending to be somebody they are not.

By repeating the activities over time, they get better and better until their approach becomes second nature. When that happens, you see managers performing some great managerial feats almost unconsciously.

With all of these things coming together, management looks effortless as well as truly elegant.

And the great thing is that, if you want it enough, this could be how you are being described in 12 months time.

I wish you well on the journey my management friend. As a goodbye gift here's my favourite Top Tips to close.

NIGEL'S TOP 10 TIPS

- Be clear on direction
- Praise good performance
- Challenge bad performance
- Don't be a flipper
- Always do monthly 1-1s
- Love your people (just a little bit)
- Never hide from difficult people decisions
- Be brave
- Be yourself
- Do it your way but………………………….
  (go on, finish it off?)

Ohhh….and make sure you get a life too!!!

Nigel

ABOUT THE AUTHOR

Nigel Jeremy BSc, MIPD, ACIB is a recognised expert within the Learning and Development profession with experience spanning over two decades. He has held a number of senior executive positions across several blue-chip environments.

He has broad ranging experience of management across a wide range of industry sectors having worked in the petroleum, finance, insurance, property, banking, IT and telecommunications sectors during his career.

His expertise spans all aspects of Human Resources and Development with particular focus on leadership and executive development, performance management and employee centric culture - what he more succinctly calls "Management, Leadership and Organisation Development".

Over recent years, demand for Nigel's services has crossed national boundaries, particularly into Northern and Southern Europe, and Nigel has developed a growing international reputation as a conference speaker in his fields of expertise.

At the time of production he was responsible for all development activity including talent management within a UK based FTSE Top 10 company. The prime responsibility being to cover the development needs of around 11000 employees and managers with a team of 70 consultants.

Nigel gained his BSc at the University of Manchester with First Class Honours, is an Associate of the Chartered Institute of Bankers, a Member of the Chartered Institute of Personnel & Development, holds level B status with the British Psychological Society and is a Licensed Business Practitioner of Neuro-Linguistic Programming.

His interests include most sports - watching rather than participating (apart from the occasional round of golf), reading, good movies and comedy in all its forms. He's also a sucker for rhythm and blues!.

Printed in the United Kingdom
by Lightning Source UK Ltd.
130817UK00001B/344/A